Cloudbreak, California

Cloudbreak, California

A Memoir

Kelly Daniels

Owl Canyon Press

First Edition, 2012

All Rights Reserved

Chapter one of this book originally appeared in a slightly
different form in *Saint Ann's Review*.

Library of Congress Cataloging-in-Publication Data

Daniels, Kelly.

Cloudbreak, California: a memoir —1st ed.

p. cm.

ISBN: 978-0-9834764-5-0

2012955200

Owl Canyon Press

Boulder, Colorado

This book is for my mother,
who read to me when I was young.

Chapter One

Redlands

It was ninth-grade Speech, and a popular kid named John was holding forth on the greatest subject ever: the practice of eating insects. To the right of the podium stood a table, set with a brown paper sack and an ominous blender. On the left, John's title, "Critters ala Carte," lurched across a poster in large, jumbled letters cut from magazines, like ransom notes or the taunts of serial killers I'd seen on television.

Having dispensed with the introduction, John paused to peel back the title page of his poster-pad, revealing a close-up of a bowl filled with fat brown beetles, big as thumbs. "Repulsive vermin?" he asked.

"Duh," the gum-chewing girl beside me muttered. The rest of us held our peace.

"Maybe to us," John intoned, "but to the savages of Africa, they're a delicacy!"

The next page featured a beetle bit in half by a grinning native, its white guts oozing like marshmallow filling.

"And not just Africans eat bugs," John continued over our groans of disgust. "Mexicans do too."

Now a shot of a locust on a toothless peasant's tongue.

"Anyone can eat insects. They're even good for you, containing many essential vitamins and minerals such as protein. To prove my point..." John fished a baggie from his grocery sack and shook the dark crawlies inside. "…I'm going to eat these raw, live crickets right here before your eyes."

Boy, oh, boy, I thought, leaning forward at my desk and rubbing my hands together like a mad scientist. This was going to be good.

John produced a carton of milk from the sack, raised it high, and poured it theatrically into the blender. He added a dollop of peanut butter and then a peeled banana. Finally, he shook the crickets into the mix, and sealed them in with the lid. He took his time unwinding the blender's cord, building the suspense. Then sunlight swept into the room, and we turned, ashamed to be caught so happy in class. A skinny boy with black hair stood in the doorway, brandishing a pale blue slip of paper. "Hold on," gravel-voiced Mr. Solter said, grabbing the note. "Daniels," he yelled, and everyone turned to me, the weird kid in the corner who never spoke.

No! I thought. How could it be? For once, I actually wanted to be here, and they chose this day, this period, to take me out. I didn't think they even knew my name up in the office.

Solter handed me the note with a clap on my shoulder. "There'll be other speeches," he said, and aimed a meaty finger at John. "Hit it!" And the blender whined like a sports car.

"Yeah, but not this speech," I mumbled, climbing out of my desk.

"Well, things are tough all over, kid. Scoot." He shooed me out and closed the door.

The messenger was gone, and I stood alone under the covered walkway between two single-story buildings. I shouldn't have expected anything else of Solter. *No such thing as a free lunch!* was his favorite saying, printed on posters throughout the classroom. One of them featured a mouse squashed in a trap, the cheese still locked in his dead jaws. For whatever reason, he was my favorite teacher.

My footsteps echoed off the aluminum awning and cinderblock faces of the classrooms. Alone in this place of crowds, I felt a little spooked, the sole survivor of nuclear holocaust. What would I do? Hop into the nearest Corvette, naturally. The fantasy, a common one, quickly ran its course, leaving me to wonder what I'd done to capture the notice of the authorities. The note, just my name and the date scrawled on carbon paper, offered no clues. I walked as slowly as possible, now certain I'd accidentally broken some unknown rule, and that I'd be in for it.

Eight years of public school hadn't taught me much, beyond the fact that I was woefully different from everyone else, no matter how hard I tried to be like them. I hadn't grown up in a cul-de-sac, or even in a house, a city or town. My earliest memories took place in a decommissioned delivery van, which my father had outfitted with bunks, a couch, ice chest, a propane stove and even a dresser—the essentials for life on the road. When it came time to start school, we moved to a tiny desert community called Anza, an hour drive from the nearest hospital, police or fire stations, where I'd eventually shown up for first grade, a long-haired boy with a girl's name, dressed in a homemade outfit as loose and flowing as robes. The kids called me Jesus, and it wasn't a compliment. When I tearfully told Mom about my nickname, she smiled and hugged me. Dad had taken off months before, to keep searching for the perfect wave, the endless summer. "Maybe they know more about you than they think," she said, and my tears stopped immediately, like water from a kinked hose. Life wasn't going to be easy, I realized, and no one was going to save me.

I arrived at the office and stood for a moment in front of the steel door. I pulled it open and slipped unseen into a room of dark wood paneling and short, hard carpet, quiet except for the hum of the old secretary's electric typewriter. She was too busy scowling at a raggedy man standing beside a fake palm, frowning down at *Time* magazine, to have noticed me enter. Now I was doubly perplexed. What was Dad doing here? I hadn't seen him in months.

He looked up from the magazine and smiled. "How you doing, son?"

he asked, so somber I thought he must be goofing. The secretary filled the room with the clatter of typing, and I couldn't help seeing my father through her eyes. He wore flip flops, holey blue jeans, and a Mr. Zogs Sex Wax tee shirt so old I could see his chest hair through the fabric. The school had banned these popular shirts at the beginning of the year, and the ban had made them more popular still. The scandal was far from resolved, and here he was, a parent no less, setting the wrong example. I was always half-proud and half-embarrassed by my father, just as I half wanted to be like everyone else and half wanted to be different. It was a confusing time.

"I'm okay," I said. My nine-year-old brother Ombleo, who went by Ole, stood at Dad's side, red-headed, freckle-faced, and zoned out.

"Let's get out of this place," Dad said, and dropped the magazine onto the coffee table.

The day was bright, with round, high clouds trucking east across the sky. Dad's Land Rover—a dusty safari wagon with the spare tire attached to the hood and a winch on the front bumper—stood out among the Reliants and Colts and even a shiny new Volvo. I yanked open the door and climbed into the smell of ocean, a combination of seaweed, salt, and mildew. A nub of surf wax had melted to the dash, and sand gathered in drifts on the floor mats. Ole got into the back, and Dad started the engine. I didn't know the exact destination, only that we'd be heading west until we came to water. I hoped we'd go to my grandparents' house, instead of one of Dad's crash-pad apartments, and I felt guilty for this hope. I was a self-conscious kid, often frozen by contradictory thoughts and urges. My grandparents were rich, Dad was poor. I'd learned that wealth made you weak, soft, and blind to reality, but I couldn't help myself. I liked swimming in the big pool, shopping for a new bicycle or video games or the sneakers and jeans and polo shirts that all the other kids were wearing; I liked eating sugary cereal and ice cream on the giant couch while watching the giant television.

Ten miles down the freeway, Dad still hadn't explained why he'd pulled us from school. He was in a dark mood, so I didn't press. It had taken almost an hour while the principal, "Mean" Dr. Green, called my mother, checked Dad's ID and generally made a production out of excusing me from class. "Just another little man on a power trip," Dad said to no one, and laughed a bit.

"Well," I said, "thanks for busting me loose."

I hoped for a quip in response, one of his warnings to never trust what they taught me in school, but Dad only looked at me and smiled in this sad, disappointed way he had. We rose onto the big bowtie junction that led from the 10 to the 91, way above low-flung San Bernardino. A blanket of brown haze lay across the land, hiding even the nearby mountains. Aside from the Ferris wheel of a traveling carnival, all I could see were small boxy buildings, tangles of power lines, and cars moving along an infinite grid of streets. We coasted back to earth and drove on, silent except for the rattle of the Rover's engine, the hum of tires, and the wind whistling through old window seals.

We passed through Riverside, then Corona, and into an undeveloped stretch that marked a transition from the Inland Empire to Orange County. A shallow river valley followed the freeway to the right, full of sparkling green trees. Bare brown hills rose on the left. I nestled into the seat and yawned, lulled by the familiar rhythm of freeway travel.

"I figured you should hear it from me first," Dad said, and cleared his throat. "Instead of reading about it in the paper, or whatever."

I opened my eyes and saw him wince at the windshield, as if he'd bitten into a lemon.

"They say I thought Barclay was sleeping with Julie, but that's not it."

I had no idea what he was talking about. Julie was his new wife, a woman I'd only met a few times. I knew Barclay by name, a cousin of my father's who had some money.

"I remember," he said, staring intently forward and gripping the wheel so hard the veins bulged from his forearms, "I remember thinking about how many lives that man had ruined, and then I woke up in jail with a real bad feeling. For a while…" He chuckled grimly, shaking his head.

For a while, what? Did he say jail? My heart began to pound, and my stomach gurgled.

"To be honest, it was kind of a relief when the guard finally told me I killed Barclay."

We drove in silence long enough for the words to take on their meanings. He turned to me, a pale-eyed man with a round Irish face, roughed up by the sun. "You can cry if you want," he said.

I blinked hard and looked away, surprised by his words. I placed my hand over my mouth to hide a giddy smile creeping into my face.

"I don't want to make excuses," he said, "but Barclay wasn't a good man."

The air in the Rover began to shimmer, and everything went strangely vivid. Dad's voice didn't travel through the space between us; it was just there in my head. Meanwhile, the other sounds—engine, tires, wind— came hushed, as if through a thick bubble of glass. The wax on the dashboard appeared distant and huge, like something you travel to visit, climbing over the contours and cracks on the dash to get to that mound of frozen melt. The long, angled stick shift was the same, an outrageous landmark. I too was giant, the hand on my lap carved from a mountain to the scale of Rushmore. I looked out the window, and the world revealed itself as false, a movie set thrown together just for this moment. The cars speeding by were driven by actors pretending not to notice what was going on. The trees and the sky were painted onto screens. I covered my face in my hands to contain the maniac laughter bubbling in my chest. Oh no, I wasn't going to cry. The opposite. I felt wonderful. I know this sounds strange, even cold-blooded, but that's the right word. Full of wonder. I'd become an actor playing myself in the movie about my life, and I knew nothing was ever going to be the same again.

CLOUDBREAK, CALIFORNIA

I recalled meeting Barclay once before. I pictured a stocky outline, dark hair, a suit. Ole, Dad, and I had gone to a sushi restaurant somewhere in the concrete interior of Orange County—Santa Ana or Anaheim or Orange, one of those inland cities that all blended together in my mind. It had been daytime, very bright in the strip mall parking lot, and so dark in the restaurant it took a minute for the eyes to adjust. The place had been empty, or nearly so. Dad, another man, and Barclay sat at a booth, drinking and talking grownup talk, which meant drug-dealer talk. Dad put Ole and I two booths away, so we wouldn't hear something we might innocently repeat. The waitress had instructions to keep the Roy Rogers coming, Coke with grenadine and a cherry, served in smoky highball glasses with red straws. Little desert-dwelling animals that we were in those days, we couldn't help gobbling the cherries and sucking down the sugar water as quickly as they came. Before long, we'd gulped several drinks each. Throbbing with sugar and caffeine, confined to a quiet booth, we began to stare at each other, and to giggle. Nothing was funny, except that we weren't allowed to laugh. Finally, Dad had to come to our table and give us the disappointed face. "You guys all right?" he'd finally asked. "Think you can cool it a little longer?" We said we could, and he returned to the grownup table. For a while, we managed to keep it together, but the hilarity began to build again, like pressure in a shaken bottle. We clamped shut our mouths to hold it in, but then I squeaked out a fart and we lost it big time.

That was my only memory of Barclay, and it didn't live up to the moment.

A concrete dam, painted red, white, and blue in honor of the American Bicentenial, bottled up the river, and the ammonia smell from nearby dairy farms crept in through the cracks in the Rover. "One other thing," Dad said, looking directly at me. "Barclay's got a son your age. Used to at least. Anyway. I'm sorry to lay this on you, but I'm not going to be around to watch your back. This kid may come after you someday, to get back at me. You're going to have to look after yourself. You understand what I'm saying?"

I nodded dumbly as we drifted onto the 55, under a sign that read "Beach Cities," quiet now except for Ole's gentle sobs from the back seat.

◆

We spent the rest of the week at my grandparents' place in Laguna, a hillside estate with a pool, Jacuzzi, a series of koi fish ponds fed by waterfalls, and an ocean view from nearly every window of the sprawling ranch-style house. I loved it here. Who wouldn't? It was my time to be a rich kid, pampered by grandma Helen and roughhoused by grandpa Gil for a couple of weeks at a time, before being sent back to Mom and varying degrees of poverty. Toward the end of the Anza years, Mom threw her lot in with the Church of the Living Word—a nondenominational church that I'd later find profiled in a book called the *Cults of North America*. To be nearer the church, we moved from our cabin in Anza to a nowhere-town off the 15 freeway, into a single-wide trailer that still smelled of the piss left by the cat-lady former owner. From there, we visited several congregations—called "bodies" in church lingo—until we finally settled in Redlands, a dusty city of 50,000 an hour east of Los Angeles, where we lived with a roommate in a tiny one-bedroom apartment on a street populated by bikers and other rough sorts. The elders put Mom to work, without pay, as a seamstress in the church-owned clothing factory, while helping her apply for welfare and food stamps. This situation lasted a couple of years, until Mom— with the church's counsel and permission—married Ralph, a former chopper rider who now made a good living working for the phone company. This is all to say that Ole and I usually loved getting spoiled by Grandma and Grandpa, but today we wandered about
the house ignored, while men in suits met with Gil, Helen, and Dad. I

was too wrapped up in my own thoughts and feelings to wonder who these men were and what they were talking about, though now—thirty years later as I write this—I understand that they'd been the defense team planning their strategy, which involved painting my father in the best light and Barclay in the worst.

On Sunday, Dad dropped us off outside our house on Orange Street, kissed us each on the cheek and drove away. Back at school, everyone acted as if nothing had happened. Nothing had happened, to them. Only to me. I walked about dazed, as if waiting but not knowing what I was waiting for. Mom had told me not to expect a miracle. Seven eye-witnesses, willing to testify, had seen Dad shoot Barclay at a crowded bar in John Wayne Airport. They'd been drinking for hours, arguing occasionally, when my father drew a pistol and fired into Barclay's head. Then he'd laid his own face on the table and slept so soundly that the police must have thought they'd come upon two corpses. I didn't expect a miracle, or anything else. Expecting played no part in what I was doing. Over the week, I sat through speech after speech in Solter's class, hardly listening, too distracted even to dread my own forthcoming performance.

But my time would come, whether I was ready for it or not. Failing to turn in a paper was one thing, skipping out on a speech another. One kid had already shown up unprepared, and Solter had forced him to stand before us anyway, simmering in merciless silence, the sort of ridicule I feared more than a broken bone. And so, on the Friday before Monday's speech, I stuck around after class to talk to Solter, hoping to catch a break. I approached the desk after everyone had gone. "Yeah?" he asked, writing in his grade book. He was a big, meaty guy with thick white hair and a red face.

I tried to find some words, but none of them felt right. I wanted him to assure me that everything was okay, that I didn't have to deliver the speech, but I knew he'd never say this, no matter the excuse.

"Speak up. Time is money. What's eating you?"

"Things are weird," I finally got out.

"Congratulations for figuring that out. You're ahead of the curve. Anything else?" He looked up from his grade book, a square-faced man who smelled like menthol shaving cream, the kind I'd been experimenting with. The jacket he always wore had patches on the elbows. I couldn't picture him ever having been young.

"No," I said. "Nothing else. See you Monday."

"Kid," he called as I walked away. "Surprise yourself. Everybody's got something to say. You just have to find it and let it out."

I thought the rest of the day about what it was I had to say, and kept thinking on the long bike ride home. I bunny hopped a curb, entered the alley behind Ralph's place—now our place—and rode through the listing wooden gate into the back yard. All the worry had worn me out, and the answer seemed farther away than ever. I hadn't come up with a single idea.

Mom sat wedged into a corner of the new sectional couch she and Ralph had gotten as a wedding present, reading one of her Conan novels. She'd recently cut her long, straight hair into the feathery style of Dorothy Hamill, a famous figure skater of the time. I wasn't used to the new hair, the new house, or the new step father, and Mom seemed for a moment like someone else's mother, or rather, everyone else's mother, one of the women who picked her kids up at school. The problem was that I wasn't one of those kids. "Come here," she said, patting a cushion, the book on her lap.

I sat beside her, staring at my reflection on the blank TV screen.

"Your father's gone," she said.

"Gone?" I was still watching myself, not her.

"He jumped bail."

"Where'd he go?" I asked.

She reached over and touched my head. "Nobody knows. If they knew, they'd catch him."

"Okay," I said, and stood. I wasn't sure how to feel, so I chose to take the news as routine information, as if church had been switched from Wednesday to Thursday.

"Don't worry about him. He's surfing out there somewhere. He'll be fine. He always is."

I could hear the anger in her voice, but paid it no mind. She always sounded like that when talking about my dad.

"How about you?" she asked. "Are you alright?"

"Yes," I said. "I have to give a speech on Monday."

"Well, keep up with your homework. You don't want to fall behind. Listen. I know it's hard, but try not to think about your father too much, if you can. He can't come back."

I went into my room and closed the door. An old rabbit pelt, stiff and smelly, lay on my desk, a mat on which to display my Pinewood Derby car and the first-place trophy it had earned, the only thing I'd ever won. I'd shot the rabbit myself, in Anza that summer I'd stayed with Dad, after Mom and I had moved away, and Dad had moved back in. At first I couldn't understand why he'd taken our place like that, especially since he'd originally left because there wasn't any surf in Anza. I'd begun to suspect that it must have been us who had driven him away, but then I stumbled upon his pot crop in the Manzanita grove and understood. He was here to grow weed.

We went hunting on a lark, to practice shooting the rifles he'd bought so he could better protect the crop. With an old, crappy .22, I'd hit a jackrabbit from a hundred yards away, an amazing, lucky shot way over onto the Cahuilla Reservation that bordered our property. We'd meant to cook whatever we killed for dinner, especially after Dad's lecture about how disrespectful it was to waste an animal, one shot on Indian land no less. But his girlfriend at the time called it a rodent and refused to let us bring it into the kitchen. Trying to salvage the situation, to convince myself that the act meant something, I insisted we cure the hide, imagining making a hat of it or something nice for my mom. Dad wasn't so sure, but he helped me skin the animal, and then he nailed the pelt to a piece of plywood. As an afterthought, he sprinkled on some of his dog's flea powder. Over the next days, the skin dried into a crusty tray, and though I realized we hadn't done it right, that Dad didn't actually know how to make the fur soft like it should be, I brought it home anyway, and had kept it through several moves. Only now was I beginning to accept it for what it was, worthless and dirty.

My notebook lay open to a blank page, and I could find no words to put on it. I crossed the hall to Mom and Ralph's room, which was dark with the blinds drawn. I faced the full-length mirror and didn't like what I saw. Bi-level hair cut in straight lines, one at the forehead and the other at the collar, just curly enough for wavelets to shoot up here and there, no matter how often I wet them and combed them down. Tan velour pullover, stained right down the center as if from drool. Baggy corduroy pants, Hush Puppy shoes, big front teeth gapped in the middle. Not cool. The girls didn't like me. The boys didn't either. At best, I was ignored, but they can't ignore you when you stand at the front of the class and give a speech.

It had always been my habit to avoid bad thoughts, but I couldn't dodge them now, so I gave in; I pictured, I dwelled. My zipper's down. Pretty Kathleen Connor sneers. Everybody laughs, passes notes. I stutter. Giant sweat stains appear under my arms. I forget how to read. I freeze. The minutes tick by. Solter gives me an F.

Okay, I thought, squinting at the kid in the mirror. I licked my dry lips and stepped closer, heart pounding. A cool wave moved from my scalp down to my toes, waking me up as if from a groggy dream. I didn't care what they thought, not anymore, and maybe never again. I knew something they didn't know. I was somebody they didn't know, and they weren't going to know me, not unless I wanted them to, not unless I let them. Who were they, anyway? Nobodies. Regular boys and girls with regular fathers and mothers who lived in regular houses where nothing ever happened. And who was I? Well, I had secrets, and secrets within secrets. My father was a fugitive, an outlaw at large, sure. A look in the newspaper could tell you that. But there was more to it. A boy, my age, a hidden enemy, was growing up alongside me, plotting revenge. I'd never met him, but he was out there, living as I lived, walking through grass, sitting at desks, thinking about the escaped man who killed his father, and then thinking about me, that man's son.

A gray, hound's-tooth cap hung on the door behind me, the English type that snaps down low onto the brim. A famous television detective wore a hat like that. I fit it on my head, and though it was too large, I kept it on as I slipped out of the house without Mom noticing, walked away from home and into the neighborhood west of Orange Street to the part of town I was supposed to avoid. In a quiet park of cracked basketball courts and grass covered in dandelions, I studied the graffiti etched across the handball court, as if trying to crack a code. The dozen cholos standing around a low-rider in the parking lot ignored me. For all they knew, I was exactly where I was supposed to be.

I ventured down a narrow street, padding silently in my Hush Puppies, noticing parked cars and people on porches and bits of trash caught in sewer drains, strolling casually as if I hadn't noticed anything at all. In a flash, I ducked into an alley and, halfway to the end, cut up between two houses and back onto another street, shaking my invisible stalker. Trouble would find me one day, and when it did, I was going to have to be ready.

And that's not all I'd be ready for. Mom told me to forget him, but I wasn't going to. I held one final secret, even from those who knew the rest. One of these days, the message would arrive. It might not come for five years, ten years, twenty years, but someday it would find its way into my hands: a puzzle, a riddle, sketches and lines and arrows and Xs and Os; a map. I'd study it, break the code. Then I'd cross borders, cross the ocean. I'd find the uncharted island, hack through jungle to the hidden cove where out in the water a lone man surfed glassy waves like the ones printed on tee shirts, the ones I'd seen him surf in the mist of dawn. I'd lift the spare board from the sand and paddle out. We'd sit like cowboys on our mounts, not talking, just watching the horizon for waves as the sun rose over the water.

◆

Sunday after church, watching the Rams on television with Ralph, I began to compose the speech, about football of all things. I'd taken an interest in strategy of late, in offense, defense, Xs and Os. I jotted some notes, came up with an introduction, a conclusion, a few plays to fit in the middle. The next day, I carried the papers up to the podium, tilted the detective cap low to hide my eyes and began to read. After I'd gotten through the introduction, I pushed the cap high on the forehead and regarded them, my fellow students. They looked pretty and handsome and knew how to dress, how to act, what to say and when to say it; they understood parties, dancing, and what music to listen to, but I wasn't afraid of them. I drew Xs on one side of the board; I drew Os on the other. I drew lines and arrows. Offense, defense. Cat and mouse. They run this way, you run that. It's simple, I explained. Solter gave me an A, but I didn't care about the grade. I had other worries.

Chapter Two

San Francisco

I brought it up over dinner. It was October, ten years after my father's disappearance, and I sat on the bed with my girlfriend Rachel, watching television and eating what had become a regular meal. A recent backpacking trip through Europe had given me a taste for picnic fare, so I often returned from work with salamis, jars of olives, fruit, cheese, a baguette, all of which I'd spread across a cutting board while Rachel draped a sheet over the bed. We'd sit cross legged with our backs to the wall, munching and flipping channels. Rachel was into sitcoms, and I preferred news. We took turns getting what we wanted. On this particular evening we watched a big, calm face talking about last year's riots in Los Angeles.

"How long will you be gone?" Rachel asked, sawing through a block of cheddar.

"A couple months I guess. Something like Europe. Maybe longer."

"Two months in Central America, huh? Why there?"

"I don't know. Practice Spanish. It's cheap. I've already been to Mexico. No particular reason." In truth, I wasn't sure myself; I just wanted to go somewhere, do something, and the fact that I would graduate from college next spring—the only one in my family who'd ever done anything like that—seemed a good enough excuse. This restlessness was nothing new. Throughout high school I'd often watched the freight trains rattling through town, dreaming. One of these days, I'd hop onto a boxcar and go wherever it took me. Or I'd hitch a ride to the Mexican border and cross over, never to be seen in this country again. Or I'd move to Hollywood, make it as a rock star or die trying. I'd join a sailing crew, take pictures for *National Geographic*, become an anthropologist and discover lost tribes.

"And I'll just stay here?" Rachel asked.

"Sure," I said, surprised by the question. "I mean, you can come if you want." I pictured her stepping from a rusty old bus into a jungle village, shiny yellow hair with the tips of her ears poking through like buds from soil, backpack laden with unguents and ornamental shoes.

"No," she said. "I'd better stick around, hold down the fort."

"If that's what you want. It's up to you."

I caught her gesturing noncommittally out of the corner of my eye. I closed my eyes against the familiar clip of a black rioter smashing a white truck driver's skull with a brick and then dancing around in glee. When I opened my eyes, the newsreader's placid face had returned to the screen, explaining how, a year after the riots and in spite of many promises by important people, nothing had changed in Los Angeles. It occurred to me that what I wanted was for Rachel to send me off forever. The sudden desire took my breath away, and I rejected it as a faulty impulse, the old demon in me that loved to throw things away. Somewhere along the line, I'd gotten addicted to what I thought of as freedom, which meant I tended to avoid or shed every last encumbrance; I'd gotten used to loneliness, and even took a masochistic pleasure from it. But I was, as always, conflicted. I didn't want to be the person I used to be, and I didn't want to lose Rachel. She was good for me.

We'd met last May, three weeks before I was to leave for a summer trip through Europe—the most anticipated event in my life up to that point. During the truncated courtship, or because of it, we'd rashly agreed to move in together upon my return. So far, after three months in a room in a Victorian flat with a couple of roommates, we'd gotten along just fine. When feeling bored and cloistered, I'd remind myself that this was real life, adult life, sharing space and chores with a woman who causes no trouble, a decent person who didn't drive me nuts, didn't keep me up late with jealous worry or fights, a woman who didn't send my heart into scary palpitations. I'd had that before, and by the end, the pain had measured equally to the ecstasy. No such thing as a free lunch, as Solter would say.

"We'll talk about it later," I said, hatching a new plan. Upon graduation, I'd surprise Rachel with a vacation to Cabo San Lucas, or some such poolside resort, spend whatever I managed to save on one short burst of luxury instead of months of lonely wandering.

"Whatever you decide," she said, and the phone rang. The one on my nightstand was an old-fashioned rotary model I'd found at a garage sale, hotline red with a shrill bell, actual metal banging on metal. Ninety percent of the time it was for one of the roommates, so I wasn't in a hurry to answer.

"What do you think it'll take to fix L.A.?" I asked.

"I don't know," she said. "I wasn't paying attention. Are you going to get that?"

I picked up the phone as looters poured from the broken windows of an electronics store, televisions and stereos in their arms. "Hello?"

"They have your father." It took me a moment to recognize the voice as my grandmother's. It took me more moments to process what she'd said.

"Did you hear me? Are you there?"

"How?" I managed to get out.

"They picked him up in the Philippines. He's in Orange County Jail now. I'm going as soon as I get off the phone."

I stammered, trying to get to all the questions at once. Where? Why? With whom? Doing what?

"We better not talk over the phone," she said, and hung up. Helen had long believed her line to be tapped, and when I lived with her a couple of years before moving to San Francisco—during my transition from unemployed couch-surfing drywall-hanger to table-waiting college-student—she would frequently warn me to be careful when making calls. "Why?" I'd ask. "What do I have to worry about? What do I even know?"

Her fears weren't totally unfounded. One morning toward the end of my stay in Laguna, but before I'd been accepted and funded at San Francisco State, the doorbell woke me into a hangover. I ran my tongue over my chapped lips, rolled out of bed, and went downstairs to the door. A tall man in a suit stood there scribbling onto a notepad. He was in his sixties, with gray hair parted far to one side and sprayed down neatly against his skull, more gentleman than cop. "Good morning," he said. "I'm agent Schroeder with the FBI. May I speak to Helen Hodges?" I told him my grandparents weren't home. He scribbled something onto his note pad, then asked if he could come in and ask me a few questions.

I had nothing to hide, except the alcohol oozing from my pores, my blurred vision, queasy stomach, and last night's waiter clothes I'd slept in. I led agent Schroeder into the living room, suddenly embarrassed by the opulence, the ancient Chinese chairs made of paper *mâché* inlaid with abalone, the twelve-foot arched windows looking out on private Three Arch Bay. I saw myself through his eyes, a spoiled kid, longhaired back then, drunk and living off Grandma and Grandpa. Like father like son. I wanted to protest, to explain that I hadn't grown up like this, that I'd been poor more often than rich, but in the end I had to just let him believe what he believed. He asked my name, where I worked, what I studied at the community college, and then he got to business. "Do you know where your father is?"

"No."

"Do your grandparents know where your father is?"

"No."

He smiled a bit, a sly grin. "I'm trained to detect when someone lies, and you just lied."

This caught me off guard. Most people don't call other people liars, not casually, not while smiling. "I'm comfortable with my innocence," I finally said, and this was the truth. I'd done many shameful things in my life, but refusing to indict my grandparents wasn't one of them. He thanked me for my time and that was the last I heard from the feds.

Placing the phone gently onto the receiver, I felt Rachel watching me. I climbed off the bed, careful not to disturb the food, careful not to meet her gaze. "Are you okay?" she asked, and I punched a hole into the drywall. "Oh my God," she said, and I wheeled on her.

"Don't," I said quietly. "Please. Don't say another word."

I walked out of the room and out of the house and down the street, through habit heading toward the bus that took me to work. At the stop, I kept going, across the panhandle, up to Haight Street and west, past the begging hippies and into Golden Gate Park, muttering all the way like a schizophrenic. Finally, alone and surrounded by trees, I'd calmed enough to wonder why, why the sudden rage, why now and not back then, when everything had actually gone down? I must have been expecting it, this phone call. But no, I hadn't. My father captured was not, in spite of its likelihood, one of the scenarios I'd imagined, never once. I still couldn't believe it.

Walking slowly now, in no hurry to come to the ocean and have to decide on a new course, I considered what awaited me. Instead of finding him on that mythical tropical island some sunny day in a future that would never come, I'd visit him in prison, staving off thoughts of the violence and humiliation that went on in those places. How would they treat a small, aging man? Not kindly. I knew a little about prison, from a family member's perspective. Ole, once with a shortstop's frame like mine but now grown to a muscle-bound, tattooed hulk, had recently been released from Pelican Bay, a prison that had once denied my request for a visit, on the grounds that I was considered an accomplice. This made no sense. I'd had no connection with my brother in years. Furthermore, if I were an accomplice, why hadn't I ever been arrested, charged, tried, or in any way investigated? My questions were moot. The prison didn't answer to me, or, for all I knew, anyone.

Would I accept the paperwork, body searches, the smelly waiting rooms, the long hours wasted, or would I stomach the guilt and abandon him to his little hell? He hadn't, in the final count, given me much. Not even the modest child support ordered by the court. My grandparents had paid that for him. And he had killed a man. Sure, Barclay had been a cocaine dealer, far from innocent, and sure, my father had been out of his mind on coke and booze, and yes, the gun had been supplied by Barclay, along with the dope and hooch. But killing was killing. Did my father, finally, even deserve my worry, my visits, my letters and phone calls? I imagined sitting across from an old man behind unbreakable glass, year after year, listening to prison stories and watching him wither and bend until, at last, he'd be transferred to a prison hospital, to die. And only then—an old man myself by that time—would I be free of the whole business.

I came out of the woods and faced the ocean and sky, both gray. The waves stood up and crashed, big shore breaks up and down the coast like the casts of gigantic musicals bowing in unison. Only a few people walked on the beach, and they seemed lonely. My father was going to spend the rest of his days locked up, and all I could think was how this would inconvenience me.

I was confused, ashamed, angry, and I didn't understand why. But now, twenty years later, I think I have an idea. All this emotion came from sudden loss, not the loss of my father, who'd been gone a long time, but the loss of myself, or rather, the person I'd pretended to be the last ten years, that I'd hoped to be, but now never would. No longer could I tell myself that I was waiting for that secret summons from the mythical fugitive. Barclay's son wasn't stalking me; he didn't even know I existed. I wasn't going to travel across oceans, through jungles. I wasn't going to surf foreign waves, or hide out from the law. My life was no grand adventure; it never had been. I was an unexceptional man, a college student five years behind schedule, with an inmate for a father, a meth cooker for a brother, and a job as a waiter. I wasn't who I'd thought I was, and it hurt to learn this.

Back at the apartment, I apologized to Rachel. She'd discreetly placed a framed picture over the spot I'd punched. I sat with her on the bed and told the truth about my past—something I had not done before. At times, I'd considered explaining my father's situation, but she, with her happy childhood and prosperous, supportive parents, would never understand—or so I assumed. She'd either turn wary of me, child of a criminal, or, worse, pity me. So I'd lied, gave her the same story I told everyone when pressed. My father had simply disappeared, took off on a grand surf safari when I was in middle school and never returned. Just a surf bum, chasing the endless summer, the perfect wave. One of these day's he'd get in touch, but I wasn't worried about it.

As I disabused Rachel of that fantasy, the bottom half of her face smiled while the top frowned. Finished, I opened my arms, asking for a hug, but it was for her, not me. I could barely keep from recoiling at the contact. It wasn't personal. I didn't want to touch anyone at that moment.

I called Helen that night, and she offered a few clipped, spy-language details. He'd been living on a small island with a local woman and her daughter. They'd been together ten years, harming no one. Then, a few days ago, the local police came to the shack where he lived and took him away. Orange County Detectives were waiting at the station. "How'd they find him?" I asked.

"Someone ratted him out," she spat.

Ratted out? Since when did she talk that way?

The phone rang a few days later. I picked up and was addressed by a recorded voice. "You have received a collect call, from…" and then the name we shared, the name he'd bestowed upon me, his, but mine to carry, a name that often felt like a burden. And so I resented the name, and I resented the collect call, but I accepted the charges. He was my father, after all.

The phone made a clicking sound. "Hello?" I said.

"Hey, son!" His voice was energetic, youthful, upbeat even.

"Hi Dad. How're you doing?"

He laughed. "I'm hanging in there, under the circumstances. I figure this place is like a submarine, or a spaceship." He spoke quickly, like someone with the coffee jitters. "I've signed on for a long mission. To boldly go where no man has gone before. We'll eventually come back to land, or back to Earth. Whichever. I just got to hang tight for a while. It's going to be a real trip, as they say."

I was trying to process the spaceship analogy, and couldn't think of anything to say about it.

"Oh, son, back in the P.I., I saw some things you wouldn't believe," he went on. "An eagle snatching a monkey off a limb. Some wild sights. A whole tribe of pigmies came out to the beach to watch me and my buddy surf. They were chanting, one word over and over. Even from the water I could see their lips were stained purple from betel nut juice. They'd never seen anyone surf before. The word meant *beautiful* in their language."

But you're in jail, I wanted to say. None of that matters anymore, your pigmies and eagles and monkeys and local wife. You're in jail and that's where you're going to stay. And where was I during all this? Here, that's where. Waiting around, for nothing.

"In a strange way, I'm kind of glad they finally found me."

"How's that?" I coolly asked.

"Now I'll finally get the chance to know you and your brother. I've been thinking of a way to sneak back in to see you all these years, but you know. Just wasn't possible. I think maybe I got caught for a reason. Sounds like your brother could use some straightening out. Maybe I've been sent back here to deal with him."

"Well, I wish you hadn't been caught."

He chuckled. "Yeah, there's that angle, too. Listen, I got to go. Some guys are waiting to use the phone. Take care of yourself, son. We'll talk later."

"See you," I said, and hung up the phone.

◆

A month later, Helen offered to pay for a flight down south so I could visit my father in jail, and it so happened that I'd recently been invited to a wedding in Laguna, so I accepted on both counts. I flew into John Wayne on Friday, wondering as I passed a bar in the terminal if this was the site of the shooting. Probably I'd be able to find out, but I didn't need to know. One airport bar was as good as another when it came to this kind of thing.

Helen, in her trademark Lucille Ball wig rising like a column of fire over her head, jade-colored eyes matching the large chunk of jade on her necklace, hugged me at baggage claim. "Thanks for picking me up," I said, and hoisted my worn and dirty "Marrakesh" model backpack.

"Oh dear," she said. "We're going to have to get you some proper luggage. You look like a gypsy."

"Sure, Grandma, why not."

The Sunday after Saturday's wedding was visitor's day, so we drove Helen's Jaguar along the snarled freeways into the government district of Santa Ana. The jail was a modernist collection of concrete boxes with slits for windows at the upper levels. "I've talked to a lot of the other visitors," she whispered as we approached the double sliding doors, "and you'd be surprised how good most of the families are. Very nice parents and grandparents like me. Just decent people." She said this as if surprised, and I guess she was. She'd never expected to be a regular in a place like this.

Inside, we stood at the end of a long line of visitors, packed into a windowless, echoing hallway painted institutional green. Helen put her mouth to my ear. "I wish I could say the same about the girlfriends," she said, darting her eyes at a young Latina in a halter top, miniskirt, and platform sandals. I figured she'd dressed this way for her man. I fell in love with her a little just then, and imagined telling her to leave the loser; she was too good for him.

Every half hour we'd move twenty steps forward. Helen had gone into a silent, Zen-like state, but I was impatient, hung over from last night's reception, and irritated. It took two hours to get into a waiting room full of plastic chairs bolted to the floor. We waited in a short line and stepped up to a sliding window. Only one of us could see the prisoner, and Helen insisted I go, of course. Ever since my father had run, she'd been subtly advocating for him. He loves you and your brother, she'd claim, before reminding me how hard he worked, at a filling station, the first year of my life. Only eighteen years old when he first became a father, and small! Helen always said. She was talking about his physical size, a trim five-foot -six, but she also seemed to mean something else by the word *small*. To her, my father was always helpless, always a child, always in need of protection, and he never forgave her for this particular form of motherly love.

I know that we moved a lot the first years of my life—and now that I think about it, none of us ever really stopped moving, but that's neither here nor there. When I was two, and Dad was tired of pumping gas, we flew from the mainland to The Big Island of Hawaii, where Dad's father had gotten him a job at a Toyota factory. For a year, we lived what most people call a normal life, but the promise of new adventure—and a $500 delayed wedding present from my mother's father arriving in the mail—lured us to the island of Kauai, where we joined a jungle commune on some property owned by Elizabeth Taylor's artist brother. After several months living in a tent, we ran out of money and headed back to California, to take up with my mother's sister Anne, her new husband, Gerick Thunstrom, and their twin boys. This, as far as I've been able to figure, is when Dad started dabbling in crime. He and Gerick sold drugs—pot, pills, LSD tabs I suppose—and when they ran out of real drugs, they sold fake drugs. Soon, they wore out their welcome along the beaches of Orange County, and so both families hit the road in old step vans converted into rolling homes—the Thunstrom's pale orange, ours forest green—exploring the mountains and deserts of southern California and down into Baja, Mexico, exciting times I barely remember.

Grandma always held Gerick responsible for my father's fall from respectability, and maybe she was right. Gerick eventually turned out to be the crazier of the two. But then again, Helen always found someone else to blame for my father's shortcomings. His blood father spoiled him, told him not to listen to step-father Gil and always gave him money when he asked. The Mexican nanny who'd raised him spoiled him on the domestic front. It hadn't been her fault. Mexican women adore male babies. They can't help it. It's in their genes. "She used to call him 'Super,'" Helen often told me, her eyes shining with delight, "because he always wore Superman pajamas."

I printed my name on a form and settled into one of the plastic chairs to wait. A half hour later, they called my name—or maybe my father's name—over the crackling loudspeaker. I showed my driver's license to a guard and was escorted into the sort of room I'd seen on television, a series of booths separated by thick glass. I waited another minute at my graffiti-marked booth, and he walked in, smiled like he was embarrassed, and sat down. He'd aged, of course. The hair on the top of his head had gone except for a small tuft in the front; the rest was pale gray. He looked smaller than I remember, but his forearms still bulged with veins and muscles under the orange jumpsuit. We picked up the phones. "Hey there, son," he said, quite differently than the last time we talked. He seemed calm, if not exhausted. "How's it treating you?"

"Not bad," I said. "You?"

"Just fine."

After some uncomfortable silence, he began to tell me about life in the Philippines. He'd arrived in Managua, a shit hole, with a new name and new passport. Eventually, he'd made it out to an isolated island where he'd settled down with a good woman and her daughter. Eventually he learned Tagolog, and the locals came to see him as a wise man of sorts. "A little American education and know-how goes a long way in places like that," he said. The area Red Cross staff realized he was the only one in the village with any sense of first aid, so they gave him stores of health supplies to distribute as he saw fit. One man with an infected cut on his foot kept coming to him, the wound filthy. He'd clean it and bandage it, and the man would return a few days later, feet covered in mud and manure, wound infected. Finally, my father left the man and went to the tool shed. He returned with a large handsaw. The patient screamed and jumped up when my father moved to saw through the ankle. "If you're not going to keep it clean, I'll have to cut it off eventually anyway. We might as well get it over with." The man, according to my father's story, observed strict hygiene ever after.

"You should write a letter to your step sister sometime," he said. "She speaks pretty good English, and would love to hear from you. She knows all about you and your brother."

"Sure," I said. "I mean, she's not really my step sister, but I'll get the address from Grandma. Hey, whatever happened to your wife, Julie? Heard from her since you, you know, came back?"

"Oh, no." He laughed a little. "She filed for divorce as soon as I got busted. Guess she got more than she bargained for marrying me."

I tried to think of some comforting response, but couldn't. Dad picked up the conversation, said he was proud to hear I was in college. "Don't know where you got the education gene. Not from me or your mom. Maybe Susan." He was talking about one of his younger sisters. Susan had been working on a doctorate from UCLA when she died in a small-plane accident. She was a family heroine of sorts, and a kind of mysterious role model to me: hip, adventurous, smart, and beautiful. I remembered her rushing into and out of Gil and Helen's place when I visited as a child. In memory and pictures, she wore beret hats, hip-hugger jeans, and tall boots, always cool, always too busy to dally with the likes of us homebodies. I burned with pleasure at the comparison, and, as always when she came up in conversation, I felt the loss that I would never know her, or rather, that she would never know who I'd become.

To show Dad that I hadn't turned out a total conformist, I bragged about all the trouble I'd gotten into before college, hinting that the misbehavior still continued today. I'd also played in a punk band, hitchhiked across Europe, slept in my truck and raided orange groves for sustenance when I'd run out of money. I wanted him to know that I wasn't like those other college kids he'd heard about.

"Never made it to Europe myself," he said. "Not much interest to tell the truth. Too many cities, not enough waves. Speaking of which. I hear The Cove's still around."

Dad learned to surf at The Cove as a kid, and I'd spent a lot of time there over the years as well. In fact, my earliest memory came from The Cove. Looking back, I figure it must have happened after we'd returned from Hawaii, but before we moved into the step van. Probably we were staying with Gil and Helen, resting up for the next foray into the world. I'd have been three. I picture myself beside my father, watching perfect foot-high waves peel along the slick shore. On tiny days like this, Dad always imagined himself the size of a G.I. Joe doll, placing himself right in the tube. Mom lay nearby on a towel, reading. To the right rose the big, striated rocky point, with its gaping, dripping maw of a cave in the center. Out in the water, black rocks, bristling with mussels, burst frothing from the water and then submerged. The waves that day, at their largest, rose as high as a grown man's hip. Unrideable.

I recall being lifted, slung into the crook of Dad's left arm, while he grabbed the board with his right. He walked forward until the water came to his knees, stinging my toes with cold. He dropped the board onto the rocking surface and set me on it, up front. I clung to the slick rails, white knuckled. The board's sharp, upturned nose just managed to stay above the dipping and rising water. Dad ducked, thrust with his legs, and slid onto the board behind me as we jetted forward. An exhilarating, frightening sensation took over when his feet left the sandy bottom. We were free, unmoored. The board rocked side to side as his arms stabbed the water and pulled, trailing swirls of froth. The tip cleaved the surface under my desperately-raised chin. Cold drops pattered my back, sending shivers down every knuckle. Up ahead, a wave approached, smooth and terrible and inevitable, half as high as the sky. From shore these waves were puny. Now it was everything, coming fast, rising. I began to pant, teeth chattering, too scared to cry out. The board sliced into the base of the wave, and we rose while the deck swamped, cold Pacific water washing around my sides, spitting in my face. We crested and glided down the back of the wave with a stomach-dropping sensation. And here, before I could catch my breath, came the next. Dad's arms pulled us deeper in, as eager to meet the wave as I was to flee. This one was larger than the first, topped by a sizzling white crest. "Hold on," Dad said, and the nose pierced the mottled face. Water slapped my chest, enveloped my shoulders, my head and back. I emerged from the back of the wave, blind and sputtering, onto flat water. Blinking, coughing, hiccupping, I stared down into murk at the dark reef below, spying the intimate purple of a sea urchin tucked in a fold, the bright orange flash of a darting garibaldi.

CLOUDBREAK, CALIFORNIA

Another wave moved under us, a mere rising and falling. We'd made it "outside," to deep water, safe from the waves, but unsafe from whatever lurked below, into stillness, a gently rolling infinity and silence, except for my own shallow breathing. There we sat, with plenty of time to consider that only a bobbing sliver of foam separated me from the cold blue that went on forever, separated me from all that lived and hunted down there: squids and sharks and killer whales and creatures no one had yet discovered.

Rusty trails of kelp meandered out toward the horizon, and a line separated the blue-green surface on which we bobbed from the darker, wind-riffled ocean beyond. I couldn't grip the board any tighter, but my strength was surely not enough to keep me in this world. Dad tried to console me, but I was inconsolable, hyperventilating, "freaking out," as Dad would have put it. He became frightened too, not of the water, where he was more comfortable than on land, but of me, his young son. "Okay, okay," he said, turning the board, bringing into view the golden cliff with its jade frosting of ice plant, the familiar cave, my mother on a towel, reading a paperback. His arms dragged us back. A wave lifted us, gently from behind. His large-knuckled hands held the rail loosely behind my own tiny hands, and we were propelled forward, riding on foam. On shore, Dad hopped off the board, lifted and placed me on land, where I belonged. The memory ends here, and, as always, leaves a bitter taste.

I frequently think back on this moment, try to revise it. If only I'd handled myself more courageously, Dad would then have been more interested in teaching me to surf, and had I begun learning to surf back then, maybe we'd have stayed at the beach. We wouldn't have moved to the desert, so Dad wouldn't have had to leave us. Instead, we'd have accepted Gil and Helen's offer to buy us a house in Irvine instead of the red cabin in Anza. Dad would have gotten used to working a regular job; Ole and I would have spent our time surfing instead of trying drugs and booze. We'd have paid attention in school. We'd have good jobs, maybe families, or at least wives. Everyone would have been happy.

"The developers haven't gotten to The Cove," I said, "not yet."

"I figured it would be all hotels and mansions from L.A. to the Mexican border. I got to admit, I underestimated the people of California on this one. By the way, you ever get around to learning to surf?"

"Naw," I said, my face growing hot. "I've gone a few times, but not enough to get the hang of it. I can body surf okay, but that's about it." The last time I'd tried to surf had been about three years before, when I'd gone a few miles into Baja with some friends I'd worked with at a Laguna restaurant. The surf had been huge, twelve, fifteen-foot faces, lines of invading soldiers storming the beach. I'd spent half the morning just trying to get out, and then, after gathering enough nerve to paddle into a wave, the lip caught me and flung me and the board through the air and grinded me into a ball and left me dizzy on the beach, where I remained until cocktail hour.

"You should learn," Dad said. "My main man in the P.I., a real good guy, didn't start until he was in his thirties. He's pretty good."

"I've been meaning to," I said, and let it go at that. "How are things in there?"

He frowned and glanced over his shoulder. "Not bad, I guess. Weird." He squinted. "Sometimes I wake up in the middle of the night and hear this sound. Fists on meat. Grunting. It's never one guy against the other. Always five on one. They call them 'rat packs.' Real nasty, these people. I'm glad I'm too old to be on the front lines anymore. But these young guys, walking around with their chests out. I wish I could set them down, explain to them how they're confusing the illusion of strength with the real deal."

He looked back at a guard who'd said something. He turned to me and spoke into the phone, but it had gone dead. I mouthed goodbye, waving. He nodded his head and walked away. The illusion of strength, I thought, as I left the visiting room. The real deal. And just like that, my father was back in my life, no matter that I didn't want him there.

◆

I changed my mind about Central America. I would go, alone, immediately after graduating spring semester. The urgency felt like fear, as if Barclay's son were finally closing in on me, waiting outside my front door, lurking in every shadow. But of course it wasn't Barclay's son I was fleeing. It was me, or the person I'd been pretending to be all those years. Or maybe I wasn't running away at all. I'd lost myself at some point, and now I needed to track myself down, like a bounty hunter after a bail jumper, though in this case I was both. Not that I could have articulated any of this at the time. I simply needed to go, to move, to run. In bed with the lights out, a few days after returning from Laguna, I told Rachel about my new travel plan. After a long pause, I explained—dramatically, vaguely, disingenuously—that it was just something I had to do at this point in my life. The fact was I didn't have to do it; I didn't have to do anything. I wanted to go, so I was going, no matter what she thought about it.

"Okay," she said, her voice small but wide awake. "If you have to, I support you."

I pitied her for a moment, but I also hated her in a way, how quickly she always capitulated. And it wasn't just her I hated. I couldn't stand anything about my life, the table waiting and television, the mediocrity. Hadn't I been promised more, that day my father told me that everything had changed? Hadn't I been meant for something special? I knew that everyone felt this way about themselves; the difference, as I'd seen it, was that they were wrong and I was right.

At work, I announced to the owner of Lori's Diner, Mr. Kim, that I'd cover any shift, night or day. I needed money. Last-minute replacements, call me. The word got out, and I began to work seven days a week, often pulling doubles. I even agreed to cover a graveyard shift, ten p.m. to three a.m., filling in for one of the two middle-aged Korean women who'd been working that shift since before anyone could remember, women the other servers claimed were Mr. Kim's former concubines back in the old country. They hardly ever missed a shift, and never took vacations. I figured this shift had opened up due to some emergency or illness.

At nine thirty, I caught the Sutter bus downtown. It skirted the housing project one block east of my place, where the usual crack dealer patrolled his corner. These guys had always amused me, icons of city life, but now I detected evil in this one's gait, his charcoal trench coat. He was working for someone who was also working for someone. The web of crime spread, covering the city, ensnaring the weak and poor. How many addicts had I known, aside from my brother? I thought of my first roommate in San Francisco, whom I'd met through a roommate service. Bob, one of the nicest guys you'd ever meet, had been a heroin addict, and now he was dead. He'd gotten hooked at the age of fourteen. He'd taken his own life, with a razor in the bathtub, at thirty.

Outside the diner, three prostitutes stood on the corners of Mason and Geary, low-budget street walkers who worked the border between the Tenderloin District and the big hotels. I walked in and punched an entire Buddy Holly record into the juke box. My first customers were a family of tourists, crammed into a hotrod-red booth, no doubt hungry after arriving on a late flight. "Is Lori the owner's daughter?" the father asked, pointing at the curly-haired girl on the menu. He was trying to make the most of dinner, rallying his tired family. This was a common question, and I usually answered with a friendly lie.

"No," I said tonight. "The owner's a Korean businessman. An advertising team invented Lori."

"Well," the father said, laughing. "That's America for you. Land of opportunity."

A couple hours later, a small man in a shiny shirt and his taller sidekick, both Asian, both in greased-back pompadours, sauntered in and took the last of the column of booths. "Filipino pimps," my co-server said. "You take them. They won't ask you to whore for them."

"Coffee," the small guy said. He had a lined, monkeyish face, and a white scar ran from his ear, across his cheek, and into his wispy teenager mustache. I set two mugs on the table, and the same guy made a display of flipping through a thick roll of bills, mostly ones as far as I could tell. "Why you waste your time like this?" he asked in a heavy accent, waving an arm to indicate the restaurant. His shirt, rolled up at the sleeves, was red with pearlescent snap buttons and gold piping. The tattoos along his forearms were so blurry they resembled birthmarks. "You got to learn to manage women," he explained, laying a dollar on the table, "and you never have to work again." His friend, taller and better looking, laughed. "Let them do it for you," the little pimp explained, as if I were hanging on his words. He replaced the roll in his pants pocket.

"I'll try to remember that," I said, wondering if my father spoke this guy's language.

After the two a.m. bar rush, my co-server sent me home. Instead of waiting on the bus, I wandered south toward the Tenderloin. I carried eighty six dollars in my pocket and knew that muggings took place regularly on these streets, but I figured to skirt the district, sample the squalor from the edge for a little rush. Instead, I found myself walking all the way down to Turk Street and then right, into the heart of it. Just past the YMCA, a beautiful girl, dark like a Mexican or an Indian, stepped out from the shadow of a doorway and looked me in the eye. I knew she was a hooker, but I couldn't help staring. "Want a date?" she asked.

"I wish," I replied, a sentiment that carried various meanings. Then a man slunk out from the shadows and beckoned.

"I'll set you up, bro. Whatever you want."

I shook my head, no, and kept on down the sidewalk, past a junkie on his back beside a cone of human shit, an unshaven transvestite leaning against a car with flat tires, by winos and broken glass, and a charred and reeking couch, up to Van Ness, where a couple of boy prostitutes worked kitty corner, one of whom looked about thirteen. And then it was over, the worst neighborhood in town. I wasn't sure what I'd expected, but I left the Tenderloin vaguely disappointed. There should have been more of it, and it should have been worse.

The next day, I woke to the conviction that I had to break up with Rachel before leaving. The idea had been on my mind for some time, but only now I'd finally admitted it. I rolled out of bed and joined her in the kitchen. The roommates, both students, were out, and Rachel was studying at the kitchen table.

"Morning," she said, without taking her eyes from the human anatomy textbook in front of her.

"I have to tell you something," I said, still sleepy but determined to get it out before I lost my courage.

She had no response, as if engrossed by her book, a page featuring several drawings of an organ I couldn't identify, a cross section of tubes and holes and tissue. It had always made me queasy thinking about what was going on inside me, so I looked up at the kitchen clock. The time was only nine a.m., and I hadn't gotten nearly enough sleep. "I don't know when I'll get back from Central America," I told her.

"That's okay," she said, highlighting a passage.

"No, it's not okay."

"We'll work it out."

I couldn't see her profile through the veil of her hair, the slightly crooked chin I knew so well, the high cheekbones and small nose. "I feel like I'm done with this city."

"Then we'll move."

I took a deep breath and closed my eyes. I pictured a cobbled lane, leading through a tight passage between pastel adobe buildings to an empty beach, a scene so lonely that the entire human race seemed to have vanished. "Sure," I said. "We can talk about it later."

◆

In June, I purchased my ticket from a student travel agency, Oakland to Guatemala City with an open return date. That evening I walked into our bedroom to find Rachel staring at what seemed a dull news program on the television. "It's O.J.," she explained, transfixed. I didn't understand what a Ford Bronco slowly leading a posse of squad cars along the 405 freeway had to do with a former NFL star, but I soon caught up. We couldn't stop watching, as the Bronco drove under overpasses crowded with cheering spectators, and news broadcasters speculated about the horrific double murder. The chase ended at O.J.'s Brentwood mansion, where his son ran out of the house to meet him at the Bronco. I was dizzy, trying to recalculate. How could a great football player, an affable comedic actor I'd always vaguely liked, do something like this? On the other hand, if he hadn't done it, why had he tried to escape? In the end, I turned on him and was glad he hadn't gotten away. Even a rich and famous man like him wasn't going to wiggle out of this mess.

A few days later, another news story was brought to my attention. I was in the room dressing when Rachel brought in the paper, pointing out a small article in the international section. She said it concerned me. I finished tying my shoes and read. In rural Guatemala, a mob of peasants had attacked an American tourist, prompting a U.S. travel advisory. The local indigenous had gotten it into their heads that the retired woman had kidnapped one of their children. According to the article, rumors of Americans traveling to Guatemala to steal babies, which they then sold to hospitals to be parceled out for organ donations, had been widespread for months. Finally, these stories had turned to violence. I took the development as a sign. The universe had taken notice, and this was my first test. Would I cancel my trip, like a coward, or would I stand up and face the challenge, throw myself into the maelstrom?

"You're not still going, are you?" Rachel asked. We'd not spoken of the trip in weeks, but I'd dragged my backpack from the high shelf in the closet, and it sat empty on the top of our dresser. "There's a travel advisory," she reminded me.

"Of course I'm going," I responded, working the Marrakesh's zipper through some rust. "What does a travel advisory even mean?"

"It means you shouldn't go there. And you never even saw the doctor."

"Who can afford a doctor? Besides, I hear those malaria pills are worse than the disease."

"I disagree," Rachel said.

"Oh yeah? Is that your professional opinion?"

"It's my opinion, yes."

I removed the address card from its plastic slot in the backpack. It had my old address written in pen. "You have any paper handy?" I asked.

She sighed but didn't move. "Well," she said at last, "be careful at least. I'll be here waiting. One year left, and then I'll graduate too."

"Honestly," I said, "I don't know when we'll see each other again."

Her face went blank. She moved to her night stand and opened the drawer. "Here you go," she said, and handed me an old business card from a restaurant in L.A. "Use the back. And you better write me lots of letters."

"I'll write," I replied. "I promise."

And then the day came. I showered, dressed, and pulled the backpack onto my shoulders. It was lighter than it had been for Europe, so insubstantial I felt like running. Rachel followed me out the front door. "Give me a kiss," she said on the stoop, and I did. I waved from the sidewalk, and then once more from across the street. After that, I didn't look back. I turned the corner and breathed easier, out of her line of sight. A couple of minutes later, I was on the Sutter bus, heading for the anonymity of a BART train, and later the anonymity of a shuttle that would take me to the airport, where no one would recognize me.

Chapter Three

Totonicapán

Guatemala City looked like San Bernardino. Raw from the sleepless, redeye flight, I watched the city pass from the back seat of a local bus, jerking and rattling through brown haze and a smell of burnt trash. Far ahead, a few gleaming buildings rose over the sprawl, but all around spread poverty, low to the ground and messy. The stores and houses were of plaster, the dirt yards blocked off with wire. After a few minutes of this, the bus stopped between two junkyards. The driver, who'd promised to bring me to a regional bus station, signaled me with a flip of one hand. The back door wheezed open. This didn't look right, but I was too tired to question him. I hopped out into the street.

I saw nothing in the way of bus stations, only piles of metal rubble behind steel fences, the nearest patrolled by a silent and mangy pit bull. The bus pulled away, spewing black smoke. I walked uncertainly forward, half a block to an intersection, and there, up the narrow cross street to the right, stood a weedy plot where three ancient Pullmans sat surrounded by a couple dozen people, locals by their looks. The word "XELA" appeared hand painted on one of the bus marquees, "MOMO" on another, and "GUATE" on the third. A boy came running toward me. "Shayla?" he asked, a word I didn't know.

"Quetzaltenango?" I'd decided to start there, study some Spanish and see what happened. I'd read in my guidebook that the city was full of small, cheap language schools.

The boy nodded his head and tried to pull the bag from my shoulders. I resisted for a moment, but finally gave in. I didn't have the strength to mistrust everyone. The boy hustled the bag up to the roof of the XELA bus and tossed it among cardboard boxes, burlap sacks and the like. I didn't like being separated from everything I owned, and I didn't like being forced onto a bus that didn't seem to be going where I wanted to go, but I took heart in the kid's sense of conviction and raw competence. He deftly climbed down the side of the bus, using an open window as a foot and hand hold. "*Dose quetzales,*" he said, palm out. This came to about two dollars fifty. I paid him, and he scribbled something on a notepad and handed me the sheet. It said "XELA."

Once again I elected not to probe. I'd been traveling fifteen hours so far, on a flight that stopped like a bus at every major city on the way: Los Angeles, Mexico City, San Salvador, and Guatemala. The remaining passengers would continue on to Tegucigalpa, Managua, San José, and finally Panama City. The airline was owned by the government of El Salvador, a country that did not inspire confidence in aviation or anything else at that moment in history. The late morning heat bore down. The boy gestured for me to enter the bus. I obeyed.

Soon we were speeding through beige desert covered in scrub and stones the size of pup tents, toward mountains whose cloudy tops flickered with silent lightning. Aside from a few *ladinos* in office wear, indigenous people filled the bus, women in the colorful skirts and blouses I'd seen in pictures, though up close the clothes were dusty, the reds and greens and purples faded and bleeding into each other; the men wore charity shirts and trousers, sandals made from tire treads. A short, muscular man with fierce eyes stood in the aisle. He wore a machete strapped to his side and a tight shirt featuring the Care Bears lined up under a rainbow. The bus smelled, not unpleasantly, of sweat and earth. A faint and tender cheeping sound came from the overhead luggage shelves, packed end-to-end with cardboard boxes full of baby chicks.

CLOUDBREAK, CALIFORNIA

I was the only gringo on the bus, but, contrary to initial fears, nobody paid me any mind. I relaxed as the bare land sped by, clean air scouring my face from the half-open window. I felt light and easy, home free.

We entered the first real city of our trip an hour after sundown. Quetzaltenango, I hoped and presumed. The first stop was alongside a park of grass and concrete paths, with a bandstand in the middle. I figured this must be the central square, which I'd located on the small map in my guidebook. I told the driver's assistant that I'd be getting off, along with about half the other passengers. He said something I didn't understand, but by the tone he seemed to disagree with my decision. I insisted. The square, according to my book, was surrounded by inexpensive pensions. The boy shrugged, climbed out the nearest window and onto the roof. I waited outside with the rest until he handed down my pack.

The first hotel on my map wasn't where it was supposed to be. Instead, a private residence, front door barred, second story shuttered. Same problem with the second hotel. I was having trouble reading in the dark, and my vision was blurred from lack of sleep. Maybe I was turned around, thinking north was south, west was east. I kept searching, all around the square, up every side street. None of the hotels appeared where it should have been, and the streets weren't marked with signs. I cursed the guidebook, an off-brand publication that had cost three dollars less than the others, I cursed myself for buying it, and cursed the mayor of this baffling city for not identifying the narrow, medieval streets, lined with seamless buildings like canyon walls. Streetlights were dim and rare. Men watched from dark doorways. Shadows kept scurrying at the edge of vision. Cats? Dogs? Muggers? Over the tops of the buildings, black mountains flashed under a sky studded with strange stars.

I gave up on the map and just walked, afraid to stop and make myself a victim. A half hour later, I spied an unlit sign that said *Pension*. I ran for it and woke a kid who slept face down on a desk in an office the size of a toll booth. The cost was five quetzales, less than a dollar. I didn't take the price as good news necessarily. But I paid. The kid handed me an actual skeleton key and pointed toward a wooden gate. Through it I entered a dirt courtyard that smelled intensely of shit. I opened the padlock on door number fifteen, a mere piece of plywood with hinges made for kitchen cupboards. I clicked on a bare bulb hanging from the ceiling. The walls were cave-like and looked rough to the touch, covered in rust-colored mold. In spots I could see the faded blue of a previous era's paint job. The loose floor planks rocked on the uneven dirt below. I leaned my bag in the corner and fell onto the bed without removing my shoes. The middle of the mattress dipped nearly to the floor, and the distance between head and footboards was about eight inches shorter than I was. The mattress, I realized, jostling from side to side, was stuffed with straw. An hour later, my back burned and itched from the bites of the insects that lived in the straw. Welcome to Guatemala, I thought, rolling about and scratching.

In the blue light of dawn, I escaped the pension and headed toward a tall church spire that rose over the two-story houses all around. Five minutes later, I entered a large cobbled square surrounded by prosperous-looking buildings: a bank, an expensive hotel, the church, and what I imagined were government buildings. I sat on a bench to check my map. Everything became clear. I'd left the bus too early, mistaking an inconsequential park at the edge of town for the main square, as the bus assistant was surely trying to tell me. I bought a plastic bag full of fresh squeezed orange juice from a vendor, and drank it through a straw. I found cloyingly sweet coffee at another stand. I ate a roll and set out to find a proper room.

Quetzaltenango was quite lovely in the daylight, a city of narrow, winding cobbled roads, full of people and mules hauling carts, old ladies shouting from upper story windows at the old man selling watermelons from a wheelbarrow. The buildings' chipped faces were distinguished one from the other by a dozen shades of faded pastel. I paid fifteen quetzales for a simple room, the seat of luxury compared to my last residence. After a shower and a long nap, I went searching for a language school. I'd vowed that, at the very least, I'd learn Spanish from this trip. I'd begun to fear wasting my time, an unarticulated acknowledgement that I wasn't going to last forever.

One school seemed as good as another, so I signed on with an operation that held their one-on-one lessons in a concrete courtyard surrounded by a brick wall topped with iron spikes. Fat tropical plants rose from pots throughout the courtyard, and at any given time, about half the dozen tables were occupied by students and teachers. My instructor Claudia, a pretty, heavyset young woman whose main pedagogical technique was flirtation, taught me more than Spanish over the next two weeks. Xela, pronounced Shayla, was the old Quiché Mayan name for Quetzaltenango. The whole country was doubled like this, the names Cortez had imposed stamped on maps and government papers, the old names still spoken by the people who lived there. Religion was similar, a pagan-influenced version of Catholicism in which the old gods had joined the Catholic pantheon as saints and minor deities. The bus driver's assistants, called *ayudantes*, were considered ne'er-do-wells by Claudia and most people of substance, though I found them dashing and courageous, the way they swung in and out of windows at high speeds, stood on bus roofs like long board surfers, hopped off shouting to gather passengers long before the bus came to a stop.

Claudia eventually revealed herself as something of a radical. She believed the recent attacks on Americans were part of a plot to put the right-wing government back in power. According to her theory, hard liners had first planted the stories of organ-transplant kidnappings in the news rags the peasants read—or rather, had read to them, since most of them were illiterate—the sort of paper that relied on illustrations instead of photographs, reported on alien landings, sightings of mythic creatures like the "chupacabras," and such, papers many thought of as low-brow entertainment but which the peasants accepted as purveyors of truth. Once the notion of organ transplant kidnappings had taken root, agents— often former death-squad soldiers—infiltrated villages around the country, to be on site at crucial moments, turning mildly disgruntled crowds into vicious mobs.

I was skeptical, reasoning that this theory seemed a little too intricate for any group to actually pull off, and then Claudia showed me a photograph of one of the mobs, taken right before a violent attack. Front and center of the furious gang pushed up against a weak police barricade was a bearded, angry face, circled in red ink. The man had been positively identified as a former bodyguard and right-wing soldier, active in the violent crackdowns in the 1980s. The strategy, she explained, had worked. Middle-class voters, who had been increasingly supporting a civil rights, reform agenda, swung hard back to the law-and-order right. Distrust of natives firmly reestablished, the pro-foreign-corporation, pro-military, anti-indigenous, anti-reform party won in a landslide. The new president had been personally implicated as a leader of a death squad, but that was excused as the economy, dependent upon tourism, plummeted as a result of the U.S. travel advisory. "Why do you think so many tables are empty?" Claudia asked.

The outrages kept coming, from Claudia and from the *Prensa Libre* newspaper. Just a few weeks earlier, new revelations had come to light concerning the death of an American owner of a long-standing budget-travel Mecca in the jungle—organic farm, tree houses, and the like. He'd been nearly decapitated by soldiers, apparently because he'd refused to serve them after they'd drunkenly scared off his other customers. A day after the confrontation, they'd abducted and murdered him. Now it seemed the officer who'd ordered the killing was on the CIA payroll. After a long trial, full of unusual delays, he'd been convicted and sentenced, but somehow "escaped" on his way to prison, never to be seen again.

And currently, an American lawyer was on a hunger strike in Washington D.C., trying to shed light on the story of her husband, a Guatemalan rebel who'd been, like so many others, "disappeared." She had evidence that, again, the CIA had been involved in his abduction, torture, and murder. The lawyer had come to Guatemala to work pro-bono for indigenous rights, and had fallen in love with the young rebel. They'd been married two weeks when he disappeared. Perhaps if the kidnappers had known their victim had married a troublesome U.S. lawyer, they might have chosen another target. But in the end, no one was ever held responsible.

Head full of conspiracies, I wandered the city, soaking in the paranoia, recording ideas and images in notebooks made for school children, decorated with cartoon laser blasting robots or adorable flying ponies. I rode buses to the surrounding villages, and everywhere I saw peasants with downcast gazes, young boys in uniforms clutching machine guns, distrust, fear, clamped- down anger, contempt. I thought of Hemingway in Spain, joining the rebels against the fascists, and I decided to stay, right here, to be around when it all came down, to witness and to document.

But I needed income. As it was, my money would last about three months. Finished with my two-week Spanish course, I wandered into a gringo hangout, a coffee bar with good, expensive drinks and new age music piped through a quality sound system. Cappuccino in hand, I stood before the bulletin board and found no end of massage services, custom jewelry, pre-Columbian artifacts (poached, no doubt), scores of apartments for rent, and a hundred other ways to spend money. I couldn't imagine Hemingway scouring this bulletin board for a job, but what could I do? Times changed.

"Help Wanted," one flyer read, "*Gemas de la Selva*, producers of traditional painted furniture, is looking for a native speaker of English with at least intermediate Spanish, to manage a carpentry shop and to fill in as production manager of the paint shop as needed. Two-month contract minimum. Full time. Free room and board, competitive local wage."

It wasn't exactly driving an ambulance, wasn't exactly fighting fascists, but I dialed the number from a pay phone outside just the same. "Bueno?" asked a male voice.

I paused for a moment, surprised by the greeting. "Bueno" meant "good," and it seemed an odd way to start a conversation. Later I'd learn that this was the standard phone greeting in Guatemala. "*Hola*," I finally said, and remembered what I'd rehearsed. "*Me interesa el trabajo en la fabrica.*"

"You're American, I take it?" The voice was also American, male, with a slight drawl.

"*Si*," I stupidly responded. "I used to work in a cabinet shop. Also a big furniture factory. I've done just about everything." I was talking about the five years between high school and the beginning of college, when I'd jumped from one low-wage, hard-labor job to another. I'd never excelled in any of them, had found them dull and exhausting, but I had a basic, wide-ranging knowledge of the trades.

"Can you come by tomorrow? We're in Toto. If you get lost, ask for Ken Philips. That's me. I own Gemas."

The next morning I set out for the Gringo House, as Ken Philips called his residence, in the nearby city of Totonicapán, which was a smaller version of Xela, with almost no tourist amenities but a thriving economy based on small-scale industry. A pale young man answered the door, dressed in extra-large polyester business slacks pulled up high and cinched at the waist, a pressed shirt that ballooned out from the belt, and a large floppy hat of native material, purple and teal, the type they sold in all the tourist shops. Under the hat, Ken had long white eyelashes and pale gray eyes. I wasn't sure if he was an albino or just very, very white.

It was dark and cool inside, with terra cotta tiles on the floor and white plaster walls. Ken showed me the three bedrooms, cozy and well appointed, and an office equipped with a computer, phone, printer, fax. I met the maid, Doña Justa, a tiny woman in *traje*. She cooked and cleaned and even did laundry for management, which consisted of Ken, his production manager Cindy, and, if things worked out, me. The living room featured a big couch, overstuffed chair and ottoman, and a television served by satellite.

"We work hard," Ken said, "but we have a good time on the weekends." He had a mincing, somewhat feminine quality, and his whiteness and strange dress put me off, but aside from these surface attributes, he seemed a good enough guy, and he projected a certain air of authority and confidence. "Let's go see the shops," he said, and we climbed into the company vehicle, an old Dodge pickup.

Both Ken and the pickup defied my initial assumptions, as we sped recklessly through the narrow streets, horn wailing before every corner. We passed a beer store, outside of which several *indios* lay drunk on the sidewalk, a sight I'd gotten used to around the Guatemalan highlands. "Notice the church?" Ken asked, racing by the central plaza. The dome on top was covered in a large tarp. "It was damaged in an earthquake about ten years ago. The Catholic Church raised money to fix it, but the guy in charge ran off with every cent. Now they just change the tarp every few years." Laughing at hapless Guatemala, he turned hard left onto a road barely ten feet wide, hauled ass toward a stopped car, and braked at the last second. The car, a large rust bucket, had hit a burro cart. Nobody appeared injured, but two men argued, and the burro, still hooked to the broken cart, looked over its shoulder at the wreck, embarrassed by all the fuss. "Perfect," Ken said, jamming the shifter into reverse. He stepped on the gas and rushed backward, transmission whining. "You know how to drive a stick?" he shouted, swinging into the main artery in front of a bus, which blared its ranchero-tune horn.

"I do," I said, fingers digging into the dash.

"Good. You'll soon learn the rules of the road are different here than what you're used to." The tires squealed around a corner, as we detoured around the clogged street.

The shops, two warehouses about a hundred feet long and fifty wide, stood on a bluff outside of town. "Nice view," I commented, taking in the cluster of red-tile roofs in the center of town, giving way to picturesque rusted-roofed shanties and then rolling hills covered in green vegetation that spread to the mountains, with their permanent mantles of dark clouds that never stopped flashing with lightning.

Ken snorted and threw open his door. "Just like the Quiché to build their houses in a ditch and their factories on the hill. They have no appreciation for beauty. It has no value to them."

On the backside of the bluff lay a slum of the type I'd seen outside of Guatemala City, ramshackle huts thrown together with whatever material was at hand. From above, it resembled a dump, as if trash had blown there over the years and stuck at the base of the hill. "That's where the employees live," Ken said. "Called Chotacaj. Sometimes they'll invite you home. It's interesting."

"Neat," I said, a little alarmed by the idea of visiting that place. It looked dangerous.

Ken showed me the wood shop, which resembled its American counterparts, just a bunch of large, buzzing machines and sawdust. "We get the lumber from a bio reserve," Ken shouted over the whine of a planer. "Everyone does. You have to bribe the rangers. That's how business works about here. Hope you don't have too many qualms."

"Not me," I said. "I've always wanted to bribe someone. Just haven't had the chance."

"Oh, you'll get used to it. Wait until you get your first speeding ticket. It's kind of fun for a while, then it gets annoying."

In the paint shop, Ken turned down the loud *banda* music on the radio and introduced me to Cindy, Gema's number two. "She's Canadian," he said, frowning playfully, "but we forgive her."

"Quit it," Cindy said, swatting at Ken with her clipboard. "Nice to meet you," she said, and shook my hand. She had a pageboy haircut, round Lennon glasses and a sweet, apple-cheeked face. She went in for quality hiking boots, denim and flannel. Ken began talking to one of the workers, a small man in his forties, maybe fifties, with a long, wispy mustache. Cindy showed me around the shop, taking me through the production from bare wood to finished product. It was a multi-phase process, but the stars of the show were the "design" painters, who applied various colors and patterns of glue-based paint, much of which they scraped off to reveal the base coat below, using an assortment of homemade, personal tools kept in boxes they took home every night, no two kits the same, no two painters the same. Apparently, they'd been painting furniture this way for generations. "That's Diego," Cindy said, referring to the man Ken spoke to. "He's the leader of the design painters. The original owner saw one of his pieces and decided to go into business with him. He's been a little hard to deal with since she left."

Cindy led me from station to station, eventually coming to the end of the process, where a couple of old-time Quiché applied varnish, a thick woman in *traje* and a man wearing a curious bowler cap encircled by a *típica* hatband. "Beto here," Ken said, now standing behind me, "is a drunk. If you see him on Sunday outside the *cervaseria* you know he won't show up Monday." He turned to Cindy. "Remember when he disappeared for a whole week?"

Cindy smiled. "I remember." She addressed me. "When he finally came back, I asked him where he'd been. You'll never guess what he said. The witch on the hill cursed him."

"Witch?"

"That was his story, and he believed it. A cousin saw his wife visit the witch up on the hill, and after that, Beto couldn't get out of bed for a week. You see, Beto'd been seeing another woman, and his wife found out. Naturally, the wife paid the witch to cast a spell on him."

"How'd you handle that?" I asked. "I mean, from a human resources perspective?"

"Told him not to cheat on his wife anymore."

Back at the Gringo House office, Ken offered me the job. Forty hours a week, Monday-Friday. Five hundred quetzales a month. Free room and board in the Gringo House with Ken and Cindy. I thought for a moment, allowed my reservations to fade, and then I accepted. As soon as I signed the contract, Ken admitted I was the only applicant. There were plenty of gringos who needed money in Guatemala, but none of them wanted to work for it.

◆

I settled into the routine of full-time employment: waking, working, eating, television and sleep. Time sped up; the world shrank. I suddenly didn't feel so far away from the U.S., what with the fact that Ken was on the phone all day, selling to American boutiques. I gave up television and instead spent evenings writing, at first letters to family, on company letterhead. I even wrote a letter to my father, in care of Helen. In these newsy missives, I presented myself as an intrepid adventurer, an ironic factory manager, and I hid the tedium of workaday life behind local color. Next I tackled a harder project, a long overdue letter to Rachel, in which I'd leave no doubt as to our status as two individuals unencumbered by restrictions and duties to one another. I needed to dispel her sad specter from its customary place over my shoulder. I revised and revised until I'd gotten it about as good as I could. I folded, enveloped, stamped and sent, then walked out of the post office a little bit lighter.

Then, bored but not bored enough for more HBO Olé with Ken and Cindy, I tried my hand at fiction, a story about a gringo who comes to Guatemala—a young man something like me but taller, square-jawed, and flawed by the faint remnants of childhood acne scars. This traveler, enchanted and mystified by the country, decides he must get a job as a bus driver's *ayudante*, indeed to become the first gringo *ayudante* in history. In his quest for the position, he faces challenges and learns lessons, at least in my imagination; in the actual story I couldn't seem to get past the part of him noticing the landscape and the occupants' strange and wonderful customs, such as how enterprising little boys take it upon themselves to fill in potholes in the road and are rewarded with tossed coins by passing motorists; such as how the traffic cops—as opposed to the military, which one doesn't mess with—ride mopeds, have to pay for their own bullets and are ignored by anyone with a car that actually runs; such as Devil's Night, October 31, when trash is burned in the street to ward off the arch fiend, and nobody leaves the house except this young man—just as I had left the house on that very night—expecting a Halloween party but finding only smoke and filth and lonely streets.

November, I decided, for no good reason, to keep my twenty-sixth birthday a secret. I worked that day, a Monday, in a surreal fog, expecting something special to happen even as I knew nothing would. I was right. By the time I turned in for the night, nothing had happened, but I felt special just the same, for having kept my secret in spite of its being on the tip of my tongue all day. I rewarded myself by starting a novel I'd found on a shelf in the living room, the clock be damned. The book was a page-turner, *Talking it Over* by Julian Barnes, about a love triangle consisting of two childhood friends in love with the same woman. One friend, who first met, courted, and married the woman, was slow and steady; the other was impulsive, brilliant, in turns self-loathing and cocky...in short, damaged, but much more interesting than Mr. Steady. I identified with Mr. Damaged, and took a bitter kind of pride in the knowledge that I, like him, was messed up in ways and for reasons I couldn't quite pinpoint. I took comfort reflecting that all the best characters in books struggled with outer and inner problems, like drinking too much, falling into rages or fits of brooding, and driving away everyone who loves them. I decided

I'd rather be interesting than happy. Then I closed my eyes and waited for the alarm to sound.

After dinner one soggy Wednesday near Christmas, Ken told me to put on my coat. We were going to pay Diego a visit. I grabbed a six pack of beer from the refrigerator and climbed into the truck. Cindy got in after, and I assumed the usual position straddling the gear shift. Ken looked down at the beer between my legs. "What's that for?" he asked.

"I don't know. I thought it would be nice to bring something."

"Whatever," he said, and backed out of the driveway. We splashed through puddles on the cobbled road, past the *cervesaria*, where I pretended not to notice Beto, propped against the wall under the awning, jumbo *ballena* beer clutched like a puppy in both hands. The cobbles ended at the edge of town, and we slid through mud with the motions of a powerboat, down the hill to slosh to a stop on the border of the dark shanty.

My boots sank into four inches of mud, and we mucked across the street to a walkway made from old planks that pushed froth up between them at every step. Into the makeshift town, I felt eyes on me. Candlelight flickered and shadows drifted along the porous, makeshift walls of scrap metal and lumber, cinderblocks, loose bricks and sheets of plastic held together with wire, mud and whatever else could be found. "You remember the raid?" Ken asked, leading the expedition. The town was nearly silent, except for the chug of a small engine off in the distance.

"Sure do," Cindy said. She'd taken up the rear, and I marched between them like a prisoner.

"Raid?" I asked, squinting down at the sucking and burbling boards. The low cloudy sky cast the dimmest charcoal light down into the narrow path.

"The military came through here a couple of years ago," Ken said. "Pulled all the young males out of their houses, stuck them in vans and took them to Guate for reprogramming. Cindy and I didn't know anything about it until we got to work the next day and half the factory was absent. Then all the mothers came crying for us to rescue their boys. What a mess."

"They kidnapped them? Is that legal?"

Ken laughed, high-pitched, like a teenage girl. "It's called the draft. Haven't you noticed that all the soldiers are fifteen-year-old Indians? How else you think they get them? Seen any recruiting offices? When they run low on troops, they just round them up in all the poor neighborhoods in the country, and if the family happens to have money, they can buy the kid back, for about a thousand quetzales back then. But most of them don't have money, so that's that. We had to shell out plenty to get our skilled workers back, just to keep the operation going."

"But how?" I asked. "Why don't they just run away as soon as they can? I mean, they can't keep them locked up forever. What good would that do?"

"They get brainwashed," Cindy said. "Think about it. They pick up all these poor kids, most of them illiterate. Scare them to death. Lock them up in some big military base. Do the whole basic training thing. Wear them out, deprive them of sleep. It goes on for weeks, until they're like animals. Then they bring in the psychology. Professionals who explain how the Indian people are dirty, uneducated, don't know what's best for them, more like animals than people. Now the kids have the chance to rise above their stations. The military people let them chew on that for a while, and then the final step. They clean them up, give them haircuts, brand new uniforms, big macho boots, and finally the gun. Then it's a party. Off to the city for drinks and hookers. After that, they're ready to fire on their own people. The whole thing works because, basically, they hate themselves."

"Here we are," Ken said.

Diego's place was larger than his neighbors', a poured-concrete box with barred windows, a metal door, and a slab out front for wiping your feet. The sound of the engine we'd been hearing came from a gas-powered generator chained to an iron loop set into the concrete. Ken knocked. A silhouette appeared in a window and withdrew. Fierce whispers followed.

"Great," Cindy said.

"Wonder what they're talking about?" Ken asked, face pinched. He was all business tonight, with sky-blue dress shirt tucked into brown pleated slacks, cinched by a braided belt. None of his trademark native gear. Only his muddy hiking boots broke the illusion of First-World cubical life.

The door swung open and Diego stood there, slumped and obsequious, his wispy mustache twitching as he chewed something, probably evidence. Ken barged in and Cindy followed. I was still outside, gape-mouthed at the gall of my employers, my fellow gringos tracking mud into their employee's humble abode. I held the six pack up and smiled. Diego left me there and I entered tentatively, having stomped and wiped my boots as thoroughly as possible. Diego's wife greeted me silently. She looked older and more substantial than Diego, with her black and gray-streaked hair pulled back into a pony tail, and her jutting under-bit chin. She took the beer without smiling.

The room was furnished in matching love seats of fake velvet, both red, a Gemas coffee table, and Gemas chair in the corner. There were two closed doors against the back wall, and a purple curtain through which Diego's wife, whose name I didn't know, emerged carrying a Gemas serving tray holding four glasses and two bottles of the beer I'd just delivered. Diego gestured vaguely and I sat on one of the love seats. Cindy took the spot beside me, and Ken occupied the corner chair. Diego's wife placed the tray on the table. The design of the tray, the table, and the chair was called *Nube Noche* and featured fat fluffy clouds, partially hidden moon, several five-pointed stars, a hill, a hut, a puff of smoke over a chimney against indigo sky. Too cute for my tastes, but it was our best seller.

"Cheers," I said, and emptied the little glass in a single gulp. More, please, I felt like saying but didn't. While Cindy chatted with Diego's wife, Ken stood abruptly, untouched beer in hand, looked around as if for the bathroom, and strode to one of the doors.

"No, no," Diego said, but Ken opened it anyway. Kids. Three of them on cots, asleep in what had been a dark bedroom. Ken closed the door, sidestepped Diego as if he were nothing more than a stranger on the street, and yanked open the other door.

"Oh, boy," he said, shaking his head in amazement. "Come take a look. Our little friend's been busy again." Cindy was already at the door, and I followed. Over her shoulder I saw that the room was full from floor to ceiling with Gemas furniture.

"Is it stolen?" I whispered.

"No," Ken said. "More like bootlegged. He's making them at home, but he's using our designs and techniques. Then he's selling them to that bitch Linda Rosario for half our cost. That's why our markets are drying up. He's got no overhead, so he sells cheap, and Linda's undercutting us to our own customers. I knew it!"

"Linda used to have your job," Cindy explained. "Then she quit all the sudden. We caught Diego making these before, but we didn't know where he was selling them. Then we found out Linda lives in Guate, and put it all together. This is kind of the final piece of the puzzle."

Ken, meanwhile, had stormed over to Diego, who stood by his children's closed door, and lit into him with stumbling, furious Spanish. I picked up a word here and there. *Loyalty. Cheat. How much we pay you. Gratitude.* It went on for quite a while, and I ground my teeth to see Diego's humble silence, his bowed shoulders, while his wife stood by watching. I heard the word "rat," Ken and Cindy's secret nickname for Diego, no longer secret. Ken went on until he'd run out of words, and Diego still hadn't said a thing. His wife had taken the tray and glasses back into the kitchen.

"Sorry," Diego finally said.

"Sorry's not the point," Ken replied. "Stop doing it. Stop selling our designs. You didn't even know about varnish when Regina found you. Now your house is bigger than all your friends'. Your wage is double mine!"

"*Lo siento,*" he repeated, and I understood then, as did Ken and everyone else, that "I feel it" in no way meant Diego would stop building the knockoffs in his spare time. The fact eased my gringo shame. He would stand there passively for as long as Ken needed to shout, but he was still going to make his money.

We fishtailed through the mud, away from dark Chotacaj, and the rain started up again, pattering our windshield while I bounced back and forth against stewing Ken and pensive Cindy. "I don't quite understand," I said. "Can't you sue him or something? I mean, every other building in Xela is a lawyer's office. There must be laws against stealing people's products."

"We looked into it," Cindy said. "The designs on hand-painted furniture aren't copyrightable. All he has to do is change one tiny detail. I noticed he made the bus in *Sol y Camino* into a truck. Otherwise it's exactly the same. He turned the one big cloud in *Nube Noche* into three small ones, and the full moon became a crescent moon. There's nothing we can do."

"Why not fire him?" I asked, as we crested the hill.

"Can't do that either," Cindy said. "We've been through this before. The design painters are loyal. They'll walk out if we fire Diego, and then we'll lose everything to Linda. That's the worst part for me, how she betrayed us. I thought she was my friend. Diego's always been Diego."

We bumped onto the cobbled road and picked up speed. In the heart of town, sure enough, Don Beto slumbered under the *cervesaria*'s overhang. We'd be short one varnisher tomorrow, no doubt about it.

"Well," I said, filled with a happy sort of malice. "Looks like he's got you screwed."

Ken snorted, and I realized I was going to quit, just after the New Year, soon as my contract allowed me. I wasn't done with Central America, but I'd had enough of Gemas de la Selva. I hadn't come all this way to get caught up in workplace dramatics. This reminded me of some of the petty squabbles that took place at Lori's. Besides, it sounded like Gemas wasn't long for this world anyway. I took the events of the evening as an omen, a sign that it was time to move on.

"He's screwing his so-called friends is what he's doing," Ken said, breaking his stormy silence. "We'll go out of business within a couple of years, and everybody will be unemployed. I'll be okay. Go back to the States, former owner of an international business. Bilingual. It won't matter on my resume that the place went belly up. I'll get what I need out of it."

"He's a rat," Cindy said, but I listened with little interest now. There was a reason none of Hemingway's heroes ever held real jobs. They were boring.

"The fact is, Diego's not even the problem. The actual culprit," Ken explained, "is Asia, especially Indonesia and Thailand. Those countries produce similar folk-art furniture at a much lower price, even after shipping. You think Guatemalan labor is cheap, check out Asia. Personally, I like our designs better, but the average American doesn't care. As long as it's got bright colors."

This got me thinking. The funny thing about Gemas' products was that the original Guatemalan designs, which we still carried though they didn't sell much, were entirely abstract, quite lovely and understated in my opinion, complex in layers of color, lines, shapes imposed over shapes. The original owner, a former art major, had created all the smiling suns and brown kids waving from sweetly rounded landscapes. She gave the customers the folksiness they wanted and expected, and they took it as authentic.

We walked in and the phone was ringing. Cindy stepped into the office to answer. "It's for Kelly," she called from the hall.

"Really?" I asked, about to plop onto the couch for a dose of television. No one had ever phoned me here before.

"Yep. A girl," Cindy said. "American."

I closed the door to the office and sat before the desk. "Hello?"

"How are you?"

I recognized Rachel's voice immediately, and my skin tightened around my body. "Fine," I said, wondering how she'd gotten this number. Then yes, of course, I'd sent the breakup on letterhead. Address, fax and telephone. A stupid move, in hindsight. I'd overestimated the distance between us.

"I got your letter," she said, "and I don't understand."

"What don't you understand? I thought it was pretty clear."

"I'm scared."

"Well," I said, and trailed off. Apparently, my letter had been so carefully worded to save her feelings, it hadn't managed to deliver its message. "I'm not planning on coming back."

"Then I'll come down there."

"No. You can't."

"Why not?"

"Because I won't be here by then." I sucked in a long breath. "Listen. It's more than that. I don't want you here."

She began to cry, and this shamed me and then made me angry. "I don't love you, okay? I don't think I ever loved you. I've been trying to tell you that but you won't listen. Now please, leave me alone. It's over. You're free to get on with your life. Now do you get it?"

She had no answer, just sobs. "But why?" she finally asked.

The talk went on for some time. I felt bad about my burst of anger and told her that I hadn't meant it when I'd said I'd never loved her. I explained that I still did love her, in a way, but it was just this thing with my father that had driven me from her. Then she had hope that we'd reconcile, and I became angry again and claimed once more that I didn't love her. She cried and I tried to soften the blow. We went on like this for a good while, until we'd worn each other down. "Bye," she finally said, and hung up on me. I placed the phone into its cradle, relieved, guilty, drained, fingers tingling, a little sick to my stomach.

"What was that all about?" Ken asked. They were watching a horror film. I could tell by the music, and that a pretty girl was walking alone through what looked like an abandoned machine shop.

"Just broke up with my girlfriend," I said, imagining Rachel opening a devastating phone bill, on top of everything else.

"I didn't even know you had a girlfriend," Cindy said. The killer, wielding a sickle, appeared from the shadows behind the pretty girl. Ken screeched.

"I didn't either," I said, as the blade came down.

Chapter Four

Tikal

I gripped the ladder so tightly my fingers were white, but I made it onto the platform to join the dozen other tourists milling about, admiring the view. We stood fifty feet above the canopy, two-hundred feet above ground, and the forest spread to the horizon like the greenest sea ever. Four other temples rose from the leaves like islands, and birds sporadically broke free to sail like gulls over water. This was the tallest of Tikal's temples, the largest Mayan structure ever built, according to the guidebook. Though no fan of heights, I couldn't help inching toward the edge to get a look down. The treetops gave the illusion of a soft landing, and I wasn't afraid.

"Nice, huh?" Brad said, ruffling his fluffy hair. He looked suspiciously aristocratic for a budget traveler, with his well-fitting slacks and smooth, long-fingered hands. I'd met him the day before, a couple of weeks after leaving Gemas. Since I was already in Guatemala, I'd decided to check out the famous ruins before seeking work elsewhere.

"Spooky," I replied, imagining the ancient scene, painted priests yanking fingernails, cutting out hearts, and slicing off heads. The upper-crust Maya had been fond of a particular ball game, the losers of which would themselves be tied into human balls, carried to the tops of the tallest temples, and rolled down hundreds of stone steps to the bottom. This and dozens of other gruesome torments, meant to appease their gods, or rather, the gods they invented to justify acting out their darkest dreams. Many people had been killed in this place. I could feel it.

"It's a long drop, too," Brad put in.

I stepped away from the edge and set out to explore. Before I knew it, I found myself striding along a three-foot-wide ledge that hugged the edge of the temple. I glanced behind and saw Brad close on my heels, followed by curly-headed T.J. I'd accidentally become the leader of this little expedition, so I kept walking, assuming we'd eventually make it to the other side of the platform. Sure enough, the ledge continued on around the backside of the temple. Here, the trees below had been cleared, so that I could see two hundred feet straight down to the rocky ground. I kept moving, trying to outpace a weak-kneed, giddy feeling that I needed to ignore.

I came to an unexpected turn, where an alcove had been notched into the temple from base to crown. After three steps, a loud, mechanical clicking stopped me cold. Across from me, on the other side of the alcove and blocking the path, sat a very pale figure in a loose, patchwork dress or robe, a face so white as to perhaps be albino, with red pocks on the chin and cheeks, and dirty-white dreadlocks hanging like cigars soaked in bleach. The figure, a woman I guessed though I couldn't know for certain, had removed her sandals, and her pasty bare feet dangled negligently against the temple face. A camera with a huge lens fixed me in its blank stare, clattering like a machine gun. I looked down at my feet, and beyond, grinning in terror. I saw that my boot tips nearly touched the edge, and I fell back against the wall, molding myself to the bumps and craters where slaves had chiseled the stone. The harder I leaned into the temple, the more it seemed to be subtly pushing me away, toward the edge. I began to pant. Below the camera's eye, thin pink lips stretched into a broad, lascivious smile.

"Go back," I managed to say through clenched jaws. Brad used tiny, confused steps to get himself turned around. Now T.J. had to reverse direction, and during the pause a sudden urge came over me, to just do it, just jump and get it over with. Then Brad began to move, and I followed, focused on his boot heels. We turned one corner, then the next and soon stepped back onto the platform, where I sat on my butt as far from the edge as possible and rested my head on my arms folded across my knees. This position afforded a good look at my hiking boots. How many times had one of my laces caught an eye hook, tripping me and sending me stumbling? It had been happening regularly since I'd arrived in Guatemala three months before. Crappy shoes, I'd always thought, stooping to retie and promptly forgetting this minor design flaw in my discount hikers. But today, a loop caught on a hook up on that ledge would have been the end of me. Just like that. I shuddered, and fought off a wave of nausea.

Back on the ground, Brad, T.J., and I walked along the shady trail in silence, waiting out the sick feeling of adrenaline wearing off. Overhead, a troop of spider monkeys rattled the limbs ferociously, a bluff meant to scare off predators. The trail led to The Great Plaza, a cleared area the size of a football field, with two major temples facing each other from the end zones. The temples had vertical backs and sharply angled stairways in the front, leading up to smallish ceremonial structures on top. The effect was of a kneeling human, back straight, arms forward and resting on the ground, head high and upright. In spite of the travel advisory, the Grand Plaza was full of tourists, climbing the temples and sitting about the fresh -cut grass. Tikal had its own airport, and visitors flew in without spending time anywhere else in the country. We plopped down on the grass ourselves, lay back and soaked in the late afternoon sun.

Though its opposite in many ways, Tikal reminded me of Anza. Tikal was monumental, lush, and crowded with tourists, while Anza was lonely, barren, dwarfed by the sky. But both had a certain power, a haunted feeling. Both were home to prehistoric humans too, though Anza's Cahuilla, food foragers, had never endeavored to build monuments, or to kill each other for their gods.

We moved to Anza a few months after Ombleo was born in the green step van, parked in the mountains near Idyllwild. It had been a difficult labor, and my father had made the bad decision to experience it while tripping on mescaline. After a few hours of my mother pushing and screaming, Dad dug out a bible and began to read passages aloud, even though he and my mother had rejected Christianity in favor of "ohming"—from which Ombleo got his name—and other mystical practices that would later be termed "new age." Finally, Dad ran away, into the forest, leaving the birthing to Anne. I was there, too. I recall sitting in the front of the van, pretending to drive by yanking the big, horizontal steering wheel from side to side when Anne came into the cab from the back. "Do you want to meet your brother?" she asked.

"No," I replied, and kept navigating that imaginary road.

Since they'd gotten together in high school, my mother had made few demands of my father. When I was an infant, for example, she would frequently wait uncomplaining outside an apartment full of people she didn't know, playing with me for hours while my father partied inside. She'd often feed me by strolling through a particular supermarket, spooning yogurt into my mouth until I was full, and then she'd walk out without buying anything. But she did have one stipulation. We would settle down when I was old enough to start school. So, before I was to start first grade—Mom didn't consider kindergarten worth the trouble of attending—we came upon ten sage-covered acres and a little red cabin in Anza, and that's where she wanted to live. Gil and Helen tried to talk my parents out of Anza, and offering them a house in Irvine as an alternative, but my mother liked the red cabin. She imagined a garden, ducks, geese, chickens, a goat, and a horse. My grandparents relented, and bought the property for a song. We could live there as long as we wanted, or at least until the value increased enough to make it worth selling.

We had no water and no power. We used kerosene lamps and an

outhouse the first months, but eventually Gil and Helen had electricity and gas installed, and finally a well dug. I'm not sure exactly when my parents separated. I have no recollection of Dad living with us in Anza; he would just appear now and then, almost always to bring Ombleo and I back to the beach for a while.

Perhaps I felt his absence, but I didn't think about it. I kept busy, roaming our property and beyond. I climbed the jumbo boulders, explored abandoned shacks, trailers, and houses, or followed the deep, shady, and twisting arroyos to their ends. Sometimes I'd lie on my back in the Manzanita grove and watch wispy clouds travel across the pale sky. I'd find dead cattle, mere tents of hide and bones, coyote and rabbit skeletons half buried in the sand, dry snake skins, horny toads, and lizards whose tails would come off still twitching in my hand when I tried to catch them. The biggest threat, aside from rattlesnakes, was red ant bites. When I first arrived I'd get bullhead thorns stuck into the bottom of my feet, but soon my soles grew tough as leather. I'd catch big, black stinkbugs and drop them into the red ant holes. When they'd escape, I'd pinch off one of their legs and drop them in again. They'd struggle for several minutes, but in the end the ants would drag their victim down into the hole. At lunchtime, Mom would climb to the top of the house and shout for me to come home.

All the best rocks were on Donkeyman's property, just to the north of our land, and I never hesitated to trespass. The rocks were more mine than his. He never climbed them, and he hadn't named them either. I had. Dinosaur Rock, Racecar Rock, Beetle Rock, and my favorite, Nose Rock. I was not an imaginative namer. Nose Rock resembled a huge nose, rising from the dirt at its base, as if a giant lay buried on his back just under the earth, with only his nose aboveground, so he could breathe. Sometimes, surveying Anza from the tip of Nose Rock, I'd imagine the giant waking, pulling himself out of the dirt and carrying me on his shoulder across the land, smashing cars and houses as we went.

CLOUDBREAK, CALIFORNIA

Or I'd simply sit on Nose Rock and watch the goings on: Donkeyman, a stooped old man in a cowboy hat, .22 pistol in my former toy holster he'd stolen from our property when we'd first arrived, tending his stable of donkeys; buzzards circling high overhead; clusters of "wetbacks" picking onions all up and down the neat combed rows of the Kellogg Farm; naked Tarzan walking about his trailer up Bautista Road; jackrabbits and cottontails speeding from bush to bush.

Often I'd look out across the Cahuilla Reservation, land that spread barren to the southern horizon. I respected no border in Anza, except the one separating us from them. Partly I kept away out of respect. My father had told me that Indians had been poorly treated by whites, and furthermore, that we had a lot to learn from them, the way they lived in nature and not against it. But I was also scared of the Indians. Perhaps it was the story Dad told me early on, about how a truckload of drunk Cahuilla had recently driven through town, blasting out the shop windows with shotguns, or maybe the popular representation of the savage redskin had somehow gotten to me, even though I'd rarely watched television. More likely, it was Taquitz that scared me.

To the north of town loomed the largest mountain in the San Jacintos, called Taquitz Peak, topped by an impressive stone face. It was named, my father told me, after an old Cahuilla chieftain, notorious for killing children. He didn't know the details, only that the Cahuilla had one day discovered the dried bodies of dozens of children who'd disappeared over the years, stacked like firewood in the cave where Taquitz lived. Taquitz fled up the mountain to Taquitz Peak, and was said to live in a cave impossible to find. You could even see his face in the great rock peak, the deeply fissured forehead, the scowling eyes, the shadow of his nose. In moonlight, the face was even clearer, the scowl more pronounced, and I'd sometimes sit on the porch at night, gazing off at all the glowing stones dotting the land like grave markers, watched over by Taquitz. I assumed he was still alive up there, still a killer.

The sun sank behind Tikal's massive trees, and we decided to return to our campsite. T.J.'s penny-sized curls covered his head like a space helmet. He was from New Orleans, Brad hailed from Manhattan, and I was happy to consider myself a San Franciscan. That we'd all come from big, famous cities seemed a good reason to stick together. We had entered the park illegally, and camped in an outlying bit of ruins the night before. From the trail, our ruin appeared as a bit of vine-covered wall, but closer inspection revealed a narrow, sharply arched passageway, of the sort one associated with Middle Eastern architecture. The tunnel, long enough to become nearly lightless and bent in the middle, opened into a modest courtyard, surrounded on three sides by the building. We'd strung our hammocks in the jungle that made up the fourth wall of our yard. The rooms throughout the structure were dank and claustrophobic, but the stone roof, only ten feet above the ground, served as a comfortable deck-like lounging area. We were able to enter and exit the park undetected along a system of concrete drainage ditches.

As night fell, we retired to the deck, to talk and get high. I contributed a small bottle of rum, Brad a bit of weed, and T.J. a few dried mushroom tops. T.J. had first come to Belize with his father, where they'd bought a plot of beachfront land in the middle of nowhere. They'd been expecting a build-it-yourself house to arrive by barge, and since it was over a week late, T.J.'s dad told him to take off and explore. Brad, a bartender by trade and a photographer by inclination, was about halfway into a daring motorcycle journey, riding a Honda Enduro from New York to Tierra del Fuego while documenting the journey in journal entries and photographs. He had a gallery opening set for his return. I told them about my job at the furniture factory, and how I wanted to stick around as long as possible, maybe even settle down here somewhere.

"Why here?" Brad asked, and lit a joint. He held it in for a moment and exhaled. "Why not Spain if you like Spanish, anywhere more civilized?"

"Fuck civilization."

"I know what you mean," T.J. said. "Work, borrow more money than you'll ever earn to buy stuff you don't need, get married, have kids, retire, die. What a waste. That's why me and my dad are moving to Belize. Part time at least."

"I wouldn't mind staying right here in this park," I said, accepting the joint. "Maybe we could start up a little tour company. Bring bored Americans here to our camp, charge them for the experience of sneaking in, breaking the law. What Americans need is excitement. Life's too easy up there. We're animals made for action, not sitting at desks all day or stuck in traffic."

"How about we cut out the middle man and form a band of robbers," Brad suggested. "Steal from the rich and all that. How much would we need to get by?"

"Hell," I said, "we could learn to hunt with little bows, pluck fruit from the vine. Before long, we'd meet some sexy Mayan girls. Or at least good-looking tourists."

"Seriously," T.J. said to me, "you should go to El Salvador if you want to stay somewhere without paying. This guy I met in Belmopan told me they have these government resorts where they'll put you up free for as long as you like."

"Free?" I asked. "I don't believe it."

"I've got the address," T.J. said, fishing in his shoulder bag. "*Centro de Obrero*," he read, and handed me a slip of paper. "You just have to go to this office in San Salvador and sign up. It's one of those programs to get tourism going again."

Brad laughed. "They need more than tourists to fix that place."

He was right. Things were bad enough in Guatemala, but El Salvador was supposed to be even worse. Machine gun battles in the capital. Assassinations. Murder. Rape. "I still don't get it," I said. "How can they give out free vacations? And what's a government resort anyway?"

"The way I see it," T.J. explained, "they've got these hotels that are just sitting empty. Why not rope a few travelers into visiting, spend some money on food and beer and stuff while they're there, help out the economy. The guy who gave me the address wasn't a bullshitter. He stayed in one of these places himself."

As I mulled all this, the edge of the entrance tunnel began to glow. At first I thought it was the mushrooms starting up, but then the light focused into one hard beam, nosing along the ground before us. T.J. flicked away the roach. I capped the liquor and laid it on its side. A big man emerged from the tunnel, holding a flashlight. A skinny counterpart followed him into the courtyard. Together, they had the classic look of the comedic duo, Laurel and Hardy, Abbot and Costello, Quixote and Panza. We could see by their matching ball caps, uniforms and gun belts that they were officers of some sort. I considered jumping off the building and into the jungle to hide, but then the light found us.

"*¡Buenas tardes!*" called the big one, waving in a friendly manner. I lifted my hand weakly. "*Ven, ven,*" he said, gesturing for us to come down and join him in the courtyard. The skinny cop aimed his flashlight into the jungle and instantly pinpointed our hammocks. "Very dangerous," the big cop enunciated slowly in Spanish. "There are many thieves in this jungle. They will take your things." He whistled and slapped one hand across the other, indicating the speed at which the robbery would take place. "No camping here," he said. "Park closed," he concluded in English.

I looked at the others for support, and saw only frowns of worry and incomprehension. "There are thieves in this jungle," I translated. "They'll take our things. We can't camp."

They made their faces appear shocked by the news, shocked and then apologetic.

I turned to the officer. "We don't know," I said in Spanish, unable to manage the past tense at that moment. I tried to think of how to say "we are sorry" but I only knew how to speak for myself. "I am sorry," I said.

He tapped the flashlight into his open palm, considering our case.

"Five hundred quetzales," he decided. "Ticket," he added in English.

I relayed the sum to the others. It amounted to a hundred dollars, twice what it would have cost to legally sling our hammocks in the overpriced campground outside the park.

"We don't have five hundred," I told the officer.

He shook his head. "Then we will have to see the inspector," he said. This prospect seemed to make him sad, and it made me sad, too. I didn't want to meet *el inspector*.

Struggling in Spanish, I made the case that it was unfair to pay more than the campground itself charged. We weren't causing any harm, and nobody would have to clean up after us.

"How do you know the price of the campground?" he asked.

"It's written in the book," I said. "I can show you."

He shrugged. "Sokay. No problem," he said in English, and smiled for all of us. "Forty quetzales *cada uno*."

We gathered the money. I saw the skinny partner, up on the rooftop, pocket the rum.

We paid and promised to leave first thing in the morning. The big guy said goodnight and warned us to watch out for thieves. "They're everywhere," he said, and they left.

"So much for living here," T.J. observed, and we turned in for the night. I sorted out my thoughts in the hammock, protected—or so it felt—by the veil of a mosquito net. T.J., in the hammock beside me, began to snore, and Brad's one-man tent was lit from within. I realized I was retelling what had just happened in my head, in the form of an imaginary letter to my father. Would he be impressed by the brazenness of our plan, my successful negotiation with the ranger, in Spanish no less? No. He'd wonder what I was doing in a tourist trap in the jungle in the first place, and he'd wonder how far we were from the ocean. I moved my body to get the hammock rocking, a motion that always helped me sleep.

Chapter Five

La Libertad

Two days later, the bus left me in downtown San Salvador. A few other passengers scurried off, leaving me alone on a large plaza in the shadow of a great, domed cathedral. Nobody was out. *Siesta* time, I figured, and began to follow the small map printed in the guidebook toward the hotel I'd decided upon. "Hey boss," someone said, appearing out of nowhere and tapping my shoulder. He was a wide, muscular man in his thirties, dressed in a starched white shirt. At first I thought he wore a hairnet, but then I saw that a tattoo of a spider's web descended from his hairline to his eyebrows. "Where're you going?" he asked in English with a Chicano accent.

"Nowhere special," I said, dropping the guidebook to my side.

He laughed. "Nowhere special," he repeated, like I'd told a good joke. "No really. Where you going?"

"I've got a room reserved down this way," I lied.

"Oh yeah? You hear about them two tourists got killed last night? No? Yeah, somebody busted into their room. Made 'em kneel on the floor and shot 'em both in the head, gangster style. One of the hotels around here. Boom. Dead. All they took was their luggage. That's some shit, huh?"

"Sure is," I said, increasing my pace just a bit. "Major shit."

"Hey, what you got in this backpack here?" he asked. "You got some good stuff in here? Some mar-i-juana?"

"Dirty socks, mostly."

"Dirty socks? Naw, you got more than that."

We walked together across the open plaza, silent like a couple after a hurtful exchange.

"You never asked where I learned English," he finally said.

"Okay," I said, "where'd you learn English?"

"California! El Lay. Where you think?"

"Makes sense," I said. "I'm from California too."

"First I went up there, then I got busted, now I'm deported. That's some shit, huh?"

"Yep," I said, thinking, no, deportation after a crime didn't qualify as "some shit" in my book, especially compared to murdering tourists for their luggage.

He made a noise, a dismissive snort, as if my answers bored him. "You take care of yourself," he said, kind of angry, and then he peeled off my route.

I walked on rubber legs, out of the exposed plaza and onto a narrow city road. A hotel sign appeared ahead. I checked in, stowed my bag, and set out to find the mysterious *Centro de Obrero* office. I felt better without my backpack, and I shuffled along with my shoulders slumped, projecting an attitude of poverty and dejection, hoping to pass for a poor local, at least from a distance. If the sad sack routine didn't work, I could always run.

Two busses and a walk of several blocks brought me to the address written on T.J.'s paper. It was a smallish, two-level office building on a tree-lined street outside of town. Nothing about the street marked it as Salvadoran. I might as well have been in Ohio. I climbed a staircase to the second floor and came to a door on which was written, sure enough, *Centro de Obrero*. Inside, I found a bespectacled man in his forties behind a desk. He seemed surprised to see me. I told him in rehearsed Spanish what I'd heard about free resort accommodation, and he rummaged through a drawer to produce a half-page form in triplicate, white and blue and pink sheets. On the form were three names in Spanish followed by blank lines where I was to write my dates of arrival and departure. "All?" I asked, meaning, can I stay at all three?

He shrugged.

"How long?"

"This is a beach," he said, pointing to the top line. "This is a lake, and this," he frowned, "*es un ciénaga.*"

I didn't know that word, but his expression suggested that it was undesirable. I consulted a calendar pinned to a wall. Originally, I'd planned to brazenly sign up for months, to make one of these resorts my home, but now that I stood in this humble office, confronted by this employee in a short-sleeved dress shirt and stubby tie, I didn't have it in me to work the system like that. I put down five days at the beach, three at the lake, and left the unknown resort for another time. The official stamped the form and gave me the pink copy. I folded it, apparently my ticket to free rent, and stuck it into my passport pouch. Resorts, I thought, jogging down the steps and heading toward the bus stop. I pictured waterfront sky rises, balconies, swimming pools, hot showers and clean sheets. Oh, sure, this was Salvador, I reminded myself, not Cancun, but still. I was ready for any touch of luxury. I waited on the bus, satisfied, feeling resourceful and a little devious, like a movie scoundrel you can't help rooting for.

Back in town, I found a newspaper in the lobby of my hotel, and learned that a film whose release I'd been anticipating, *Pulp Fiction*— translated as *Tiempos Violentos*—was playing nearby. So after dinner, I joined a throng in a very large, deteriorating theater. Smoking was allowed, and generally the place felt more like a night club than a movie house. Everyone was talking and ambling about, up and down the aisles, laden with drinks and snacks, pausing to chat with friends at every turn. This behavior did not change when the film began. I was irritated at first, but then I bummed a cigarette from the teenager beside me and got into the spirit of things. In spite of the distractions, or maybe because of them, I found the movie hilarious, but whenever I laughed, I laughed alone, and all my neighbors would look over to see if I was okay.

At one point, however, we all chuckled together. Bruce Willis, having just killed a couple of perverts, straddled the vanquished foe's Harley, about to escape with the money and the girl. At this point, his timid girlfriend asked, "Whose motorcycle is this?" "This isn't a motorcycle, baby," gravel-voiced Willis replied. "It's a chopper." The subtitles translated the line as: "This isn't a motorcycle, baby, it's a helicopter." The audience roared, and so did I.

The next morning I boarded a bus for La Libertad, the location of my beach resort. I told the driver where I was going and even showed him the form. He nodded as if the place were familiar, so I sat and bumped along, watching the desert pass, my right arm hanging out the window. Four hours later, I smelled the ocean. Beach grass had replaced cactus and scrub, and a bustling beach town appeared ahead. We pulled over at the edge of town, and all the other passengers filed off. I wanted off too, but the driver shook his head when I stood to leave. Not there yet. We drove, just the two of us, down a sandy lane. Are you sure? I wanted to ask, fearing some sort of dirty work, an ambush or kidnapping, but I was too afraid of offending the driver to speak. A few minutes later, we stopped on a stretch of road bordered on either side by high walls topped with glass shards. I got out and watched the bus clatter away. I could hear surf crashing.

In front of me stood a tall wooden gate, slightly ajar. I peeked through at a courtyard, all broken concrete and brown weeds. On the far side of the courtyard was a wide, one-story building that resembled a junior high cafeteria, built in the 1950s and abandoned ever since. I entered like a thief, fearing dogs and men. A couple of palms stood near the building, scruffy with dead fronds all the way down their trunks. A modernist half arch swung out from the cafeteria wall. Its turquoise paint was chipped and faded. To the right a swimming pool languished, empty and stained green around the water line. The place felt bad, the site of a massacre or something.

I stepped up to an open sliding glass door and put my face against the screen. I saw a ping pong table on the white tile floor. *¿Hola?* I said. *¿Algien está?* A man in uniform came out of a hallway. He was of middle years, overweight, and armed with a pistol at his hip. His shirt was untucked except over the gun handle. He opened the screen and scowled. His right eye was buggy and pointed to the side. I handed him my flimsy slip of carbon paper, suddenly reminiscent of my summons from Mr. Solter's class. The guard studied it carefully. I got the impression he couldn't read. He wasn't holding it upside down or anything so obvious, but it was a feeling I had. Several times, he glanced up at me, and then back at the form, up at me and back to the form. Finally, his forehead wrinkles smoothed, and he returned the paper. Everything seemed to be in order, was the attitude.

He led me across the courtyard, past the swimming pool, which was half full of swamp water, and stopped before an enormous bunker. It was half as long as a football field and tall, with an arched roof like a jumbo Quonset hut's. He opened the padlock on the door and handed me the key. Inside were hundreds of military-style cots. Small windows high up, many of them broken, provided light. He swept his hand through the musty air. I was to make myself at home. I claimed a cot near the center, against the inland wall so I could lie with my feet toward the ocean as if tanning. I could hear the waves, but couldn't see any water, and the smell was sharp, but not unbearable, some kind of cleaner the guard splashed on the floor now and then. The windows, just below the dropped tile ceiling, were too high to afford a view.

I threw on swim trunks, grabbed my hammock, and went through the main building to the beach. It was pretty enough, a lot like California's rocky, sandy coast, but with no cliffs. Far down to the south I could see the town, a pier, specks of people, but around the Centro Obrero resort I detected no sign of human life. I tied my hammock to a rotting *palapa* and read for a bit, still unable to get into *On the Road*, now halfway through the novel. Restless, I left the book in the hammock and began to walk toward town. The shore side of the beach was buttressed by high plaster or stone walls, topped with razor wire or the glass shards gringos always write about. You'd think the owners of these houses were expecting raiders from the sea. I walked for an hour, about halfway to town, and then turned back. I didn't encounter a single person, but when I returned the hammock was gone. The thief, however, had been good enough to leave *On the Road* in the sand.

I took a swim and did a little body surfing. I'd read that La Libertad was a big surf spot, and I could see the famous break just before town, dotted with wet-suited surfers. My father probably knew about this place. I wondered what he'd say about it. It's a left, I imagined telling him, one of the best in the world. Maybe I'd write him.

I went back inside and found the guard reclining on a lawn chair with his eyes closed. Hearing my footsteps, he popped to his feet. "Ping pong?" he asked, gesturing toward the table. On it were the requisite paddles and a little white ball. I didn't feel comfortable hanging out with an armed security guard in Salvador, but I felt even worse about turning him down. He insisted I serve, and he bounced an easy one back to me. We kept a rally going for a few hits each, until he sliced a spinner that shot off the edge of the table.

"Good," I said, fetching the ball. I didn't know the word for "shot."

"Luck," the guard insisted.

The game went on like this for several serves, a few easy shots back and forth punctuated by a winner from the guard, but then he eased up and let me back into the game. I'd played ping pong before, and the skills were gradually returning, especially when the guard kept dishing up easy lobs into the center of the table. When I began to pull ahead, I followed the guard's lead by backing off; he quickly caught up. He won a tight match in the end. I won the next in similar fashion. By dusk, we'd played six times and won three each. There was an odd skill required in this version of the game, where to win more than your share seemed impolite, if not dangerous. It was more performance than competition, more ritual than game.

I thanked the guard and retired to the dorm. After a dinner of avocado, tomato, bread, and hot sauce, I bedded down. It felt strange to be alone in a place meant for hundreds. I imagined ghosts in the other cots, benign ones, hanging around because they had nowhere better to go, glad for my company. This reminded me of my father's notion of the afterlife. We, as disembodied and eternal souls, hung around an enormous casting studio, waiting to audition for roles here on Earth. In this view of things, the stories of our lives had already been written, if not rehearsed, and we only forgot what was coming by some magic initiated when soul entered flesh. It seemed as likely as heaven and hell, I figured, and then I saw something move in the darkness, as if a breeze had fluttered the veil of night. Something was flying around, larger than an insect. A bat, of course. Oh well. The place was plenty big enough for bat and human to co-exist. It occurred to me that I hadn't applied my daily dose of mosquito repellant. For the first time in months, I hadn't needed it. Bats eat mosquitoes, I reasoned, as a couple more flutters joined the first. I brought my sleeping bag up to my chin, thinking, eat your fill, friends, but stay away from me.

Then hundreds of bats poured through the missing ceiling tiles and filled the air. I curled into my sleeping bag and kept the mouth clamped tight. The sound was loud, like a thousand magicians flicking playing cards into the air. A few moments later, all was silent. I pictured the bats perched on the cots, waiting for me to show my face, or, even worse, hanging from the ceiling, ready to attack. Drenched in sweat, gasping, I finally had to risk a look out of the bag. The cool air was manna and the bats were gone, hunting the surfside night.

I would be leaving this establishment, I decided, first bus tomorrow morning. No wonder it was free! No wonder I was the only resident! It took awhile to fall asleep because I was afraid the bats would come back while I lay exposed. Perhaps they'd drink my blood. Vampire bats were rare, I'd heard or read somewhere, and they didn't typically feed on humans, but wouldn't this be the perfect scenario for the exception? At some point, however, I nodded off, in spite of my fears.

I woke at dawn, intending to walk into town, and then leave the Centro de Obrero resort in the afternoon. On the way, I paused at the famous surf spot and watched a dozen riders catching a long, left-breaking wave, about shoulder high. Envying their grace, I wished once again I'd learned to surf as a kid and cursed my father a little for leaving us out in the desert, depriving me of my birthright. As long as I could remember, I'd felt like one of those storybook princes switched at birth and raised by peasants; if I only waited long enough, my true identity would be revealed, and I'd be restored to the palace.

But maybe it wasn't like that at all, I thought, watching a surfer duck dive under a wall of foam, a move I could never have pulled off. It certainly wouldn't have been the first time I'd pretended to be someone I wasn't—so convincingly I believed my own impersonation. I'd gone through high school as a sort of amateur method actor, playing a character, day and night, I'd plagiarized from an actual Hollywood movie. I first encountered him on video, Jeff Spicoli, the stoned surfer in *Fast Times at Ridgemont High*, while sitting on the couch with my mom and Ralph a few months after my dad disappeared. The shot was of an old VW surfer bus, windows opaque. The side door slides open, and out of a dense cloud of smoke tumbles a then-unknown Sean Penn. He lands on his back, climbs to his feet, whips his scraggly blond hair from his face, and hides his eyes behind big plastic sunglasses. Then he goes to class, way late.

I'd felt weightless with joy at the sight of him, in his Ocean Pacific corduroy shorts, checkered Vans skateboard shoes, Baja poncho. He looked like all my father's friends, but better. Spicoli was funny. My hands began to sweat and one foot started madly tapping the floor. Gone was the squirming uncertainty that had been my life's default mode. Finally, I knew what to do, who to be.

I'd been searching in the usual places—sports, drama, attempts to meet girls, even Dungeons and Dragons—but nothing ever quite fit, not until Spicoli. A surfer who never surfed, a student who didn't study, he stole the show without trying, without even acknowledging there was a show to steal. How cool he was, how untouchable, how beyond History-teacher Mr. Hand's tight-fisted sanctimoniousness. A lack of effort, a slackness, was his weapon, and I saw that I'd been going about it all wrong. Where I'd been doing more, I should have been doing less. Spicoli smoked pot, and that's pretty much all he did. I figured I could handle that, or at least pretend.

I developed a little laugh, like a very soft machine gun: hu-hu-hu-hu. The other students didn't know what to make of me, in my raggy clothes, swim trunks in class, and shuffling gait. But eventually they figured it out: I was an idiot.

Funny how someone always seems to raise the stakes, call your bluff. A couple of months into the Spicoli act, my best friend and D&D cohort, the bespectacled, nerdy, and brilliant Rob P, shocked me utterly one afternoon by producing a two-foot tall bong from his older brother's closet. He expertly packed it full, and fired it up. I could barely credit what I saw; Rob was actually doing it, smoking pot. I felt like a little kid as he set the bong in front of me, flicked the lighter. *Just a moment*, I wanted to say, *hold on*, even as I fit my mouth into the cylinder and sucked. Water bubbled. Smoke swirled. Alchemy was happening in there. I filled my lungs with hot smoke, coughed out a sweet cloud, and was higher than I'd ever, ever wanted to be.

CLOUDBREAK, CALIFORNIA

I melted onto the floor and drained down the stairs into the living room, where I oozed into the fat chair and lay back, madly licking my pasty mouth and lips, noting for the first time the strange elasticity and squiggling energy of the human tongue. I chomped and licked and probed and smacked, having turned into nothing more than a giant mouth. That's when I saw him. In front of me and just under the ceiling, floated the disembodied head of Felix the Cat. It was the size of a jumbo beach ball, smiling a maniac smile and frantically licking his lips, mocking my precise mouth movements. It wasn't as if he'd just appeared, more like he'd been there all along and only now had I bothered to notice. His grinning, frenetic mouth was full of sharp teeth. He was not my friend.

Would anyone like something from my magic bag of tricks? I kept hearing in his falsetto voice.

I tried to master the workings of my mind, but the vision persisted, like a nightmare you know is a nightmare but still can't escape. It occurred to me that I might be stuck like this forever, first occurred and then became a certainty. I'd done it now, destroyed my brrain. From here on, I'd have to go through life pretending to ignore the giant cat head following me around like a personal moon. I tried to dispel Felix by feigning great interest in Rob playing Intellivision on the console, but it didn't work. Apparently Felix could read my thoughts, and no matter where I looked, he'd bob just inside my field of sight. There'd be no way I could handle this over the long haul. The authorities would eventually catch on and lock me up.

Silently fretting, I noticed Rob's father standing directly in front of me, staring down with his hands on hips, Felix bobbing just over his shoulder. He'd said something I hadn't caught. Hu-hu-hu-hu, I answered. He was a big man, a nuclear engineer experimenting with new age self-help programs. Occasionally he'd peek in on our dragon games and say something cryptic, but he was too oblique to be understood. Now I got it. I was sitting in his chair.

Rob stood behind him, signaling that it was time to go. I located my legs and rose. Outside was even worse than inside. Everything kept happening all at once. Trees waved. A man took mail out of the box. A car drove by. A girl was riding toward us on her bike. Rob pulled me off the sidewalk so she could pass. I didn't even notice that Felix had gone.

The pot eventually wore off, leaving me shaken but sane. I vowed never to smoke again, a promise I quickly broke. It turned out, the call of Spicoli was stronger than my fear of Felix. To supplement the pot smoking, I hinted to my schoolmates at a secret life as a surfer. Once a teacher asked the class what we'd done over summer break, and I announced that I'd been surfing the whole time, an outright lie. I'd in fact only visited my grandparents, splashed around a bit in Woods Cove and the beaches north up to Main Beach Laguna.

The strange part was, it hadn't felt like lying at the time—like how taking a loan wasn't stealing. I'd eventually learn to surf, just as soon as I was old enough to move back to the beach, and in the meantime, I was simply borrowing on that future certainty. But when I did move to Laguna, after five post-high-school years of failure, I found the sport just as difficult and frustrating as ever, requiring expensive gear, an automobile, patience, dedication, friends who also surfed, and a tolerance for humiliation. So I gave up on actually surfing, but not the idea that I was a surfer at heart. I managed this trick by never thinking about it.

I walked the rest of the way into La Libertad, where I found an open-air joint on a bluff overlooking the ocean. It wasn't yet noon, but I sat at the plastic table and ordered a beer anyway. With the beer, came a fresh oyster in its shell. "Free?" I asked, and the waiter shrugged. I doused the oyster in lime and hot sauce, and then slurped it down, a sensation like eating the ocean. I ordered another beer. Sure enough, an oyster accompanied that one too. According to the calculus of the moment, the more I drank the more I'd save, so I had a third beer, then wandered off to another seaside establishment and found the oyster deal to be a town-wide promotion. By the time the sun set, I'd forgotten the bats as well as the afternoon bus. I was lucky to make it back to the resort without being swallowed by the ocean. My late arrival was noted by the guard. When he looked at me expectantly, I yawned extravagantly and laid my head to the side on my two praying hands. "*Mañana?*" I asked.

"*Claro, claro*," he said, nodding vigorously.

As I'd done the night before, I covered my head in the bag as the bats came flooding out. Once the noise of their flutter ended, I lowered the bag, in time to watch a few stragglers fly about and out broken windows. I fell into a deep, drunken sleep.

By night three, I'd gotten used to the idea of the bats, and, sober, I forced myself to hold the edge of the sleeping bag under my eyes so I could watch the wall of wings coalesce before my face, ready to duck at the first sign of aggression. No bat touched me or my bag or cot. On the fourth night I dared to experience the spectacle with the bag unzipped to my chest. Meanwhile, the ping pong games continued. I finished *On the Road*, and was disappointed. It had seemed the kind of novel I'd love, full of free-spirited characters a lot like me, but I hadn't liked the characters, found them smug and boring posers, and the way they bounced from coast-to-coast seemed pointless; I felt gypped. In town, I traded it in a surfer hotel lobby for *A Hundred Years of Solitude*.

After my fifth and final night, I packed and said goodbye to the guard, whose name I'd never learned, though his ping pong techniques I knew intimately. He gripped my hand warmly and wished me happy travels.

"I'll miss this place," I said in English. He didn't understand the words, but got the general meaning. The bus came the moment I stepped out of the gate, as if it had been summoned just for me.

Chapter Six

Tela

I kept nodding off. I was traveling by bus along the Caribbean, aiming for a certain village with a reputation for mystical healing. I'd fall forward and snap awake, shaking my head and rubbing my face; then I'd do it again a few seconds later. I'd been wandering the last two months, more or less without direction. Occasionally I'd cast about for work, but there was none to be had. Tourism was hurting everywhere, and schools of all types were badly underfunded. Even local teachers could hardly be paid, much less passing gringos. Bars in tourist areas sometimes hired attractive female gringos, but never men. I gave up looking to earn money and consoled myself with less tangible rewards, like stories.

I'd come across an odd one a couple of weeks before, in a lonely outpost on the Pacific coast of Honduras, where it was too hot for anyone but fools and masochists. On the beachside patio of a restaurant leased by a couple of booze-addled gringos, I'd met a guy named Walter. He seemed normal enough at first, perhaps a little more nervous than the average traveler. Immediately after shaking my hand, he launched into his story, as if compelled or even cursed to tell it to everyone he met. It began a few months before, when Walter had been invited to a "full moon party" out in the jungle near a tiny village on the shore of Lake Atítlan, Guatemala. I knew that lake myself, a popular gringo hangout.

He'd arrived at the party with his roommate, a guy he'd met only recently. At first they stood on the edge of the festivities, a Dionysian scene in a jungle clearing, enacted by hippies gone half native, dancing about, drumming their drums, eating, drinking, and smoking. Walter wanted me to know that he didn't use drugs. He'd never even tried pot, and he never would. As the evening progressed, he felt a creeping sense of unreality, and it was more than the cold silver light streaming through foreign vegetation, the calls of night animals, the incessant drums and snake-armed writhing of the dancers, the reek of incense and marijuana. Someone had offered him cookies at the start of the evening, and now he realized he'd been drugged. His terror increased when his roommate, the one person he trusted at this gathering, joined the dancing frenzy, a weird Siamese twin-like, two-tufted pineapple in one hand, a gleaming knife in the other. The roommate bounced like a maniac, and as the drums reached a frantic crescendo, he slit the pineapple in two, separating its tufts with a wild slash of his knife while holding the tops like the hair of severed heads. He smashed one half of the dripping fruit onto his face and slavered like an animal. If you couldn't trust someone like that, a college graduate from Iowa, a biology major with short hair and modest dress, who could you trust? Now in the center of the dance, the roommate turned slowly toward Walter, knife wet, face glistening, one half the pineapple offered forth from an outstretched arm. Walter took off into the jungle.

He'd become convinced that his roommate, in cahoots with the hippies, had lured him out there and intended to sacrifice him to some vicious Mayan deity, probably cut out his heart and eat it. So he ran, blindly, scratching arms and legs on brambles, tripping face-down into mud, and even splashing through a cold stream. He fled for what seemed like hours, until, exhausted, he came upon an isolated peasant's hut, where he curled on the dirt outside the door and slept. In the morning, he found that someone had covered him in a blanket during the night.

Without returning to the room—for even in the sober light of day he still feared for his life—he caught the ferry across the lake to the expat city of Panajachel, where he paid a hotel boy to cross the lake and fetch his luggage. And here he was, still on the road, still telling his tale. I'd offered to buy him a beer, but he didn't drink.

"Tela!" the ayudante called, waking me from my stupor. I sat up and slapped my cheeks hard, then scoured my face with my hands. The bus pulled over to the side of the highway, on the edge of what seemed a fairly large city. This was not my destination, but I didn't want to fall asleep on this bus and wake in some awful terminal, stripped of my possessions. So I pulled myself up from the bench and waded into the crowded aisle. I stepped off into a loud, raw-looking city, the Marrakesh heavy on one shoulder. The bus pulled away, and I stumbled through the hard sunlight and smells of smoke, fried chicken, and sewage. Up and down the street, beat-up automobiles honked and spewed, while I barely kept from curling up on the sidewalk for a siesta, perhaps in that thin slice of shade beside the panting dog with the softball-sized tumor on its side.

I carried on for several blocks, to a gray sand beach full of sun bathers and big black vultures. The sidewalk continued to the right, and I came to a two-story building of chipped white siding that seemed to pulse and shift with the very loud Latin dance music that emanated from its walls. "Hotel," read the sign out front. I climbed three steps, dragged my feet across the lobby and rested with both arms on the counter.

"*Cuarto?*" I muttered, looking sideways at the desk woman from the nest I'd made of my arms. She wore thick-framed eyeglasses and a colorful, blurry floral-print shirt like something Monet might have painted. Her hair was long, thick, and gray. She spoke, but I couldn't understand her over the music, which was so loud the whole building trembled. She took my money and handed me a key attached to a piece of wood. I hauled myself up the stairway, rested halfway against the loose banister, and finished the climb. Room eleven was bare except for a queen-sized bed with a deep indentation in the middle and a rickety night stand. The floor listed hard toward one corner, and the music filled the room like water. I dropped belly down onto the bed and rolled onto my back.

I closed my eyes. Though I didn't sleep, I felt comfortable now, content, my body humming pleasantly in the heat. The only problem was the music. If only it would stop, I could finally relax; I could finally sleep. A stabbing pain in my belly brought me out of this strange bliss, and I saw that my boots were still laced to my feet and lay dusty on the sheet that served as a bedspread. A spider crawled slowly across the ceiling. I felt confused, indecisive, as if forgetting something important, why I'd come here, why I was on this bed with my eyes open, listening to this painful music. I wasn't supposed to wear boots to bed, but I also had to get to a bathroom. I couldn't decide which came first. The spider reached the wall and began to descend. A sound came from inside my body, a groaning like bad pipes, and I heaved myself up. My vision turned dark, with points of light whirling like fireflies, and then the room slowly returned. I staggered out the door, along a hall to an open door that led to a toilet stall.

After voiding the black liquid from my body, I hobbled down the stairs, one step at a time, holding the rail with both hands like an invalid. I went through the lobby and out into hard sunlight, already missing my room in spite of the hateful music. I'd have to leave this place, I thought, first thing in the morning. I made it to a corner store, bought a gallon jug of water and a banana that made me sick to look at. I returned to the hotel. At the base of the stairs, I had to set the water down and pause to collect my strength.

"¡Güero!" shouted someone over the techno drums. "¡Gringo!"

With much effort, as if my joints had all rusted stiff, I turned toward the voice and saw the desk woman waving me over. I nearly cried in frustration to have to walk the extra steps to her counter.

"Another night?" she asked in Spanish.

"No," I said. It was the only thing I knew for sure. "No, thank you."

She looked at me through those big glasses, irritated, even hostile. "Then you have to leave," she said. Her irises were entirely black. I didn't understand. Had I done something wrong? "Checkout is twelve," she explained, pointing to a clock whose numbers and hands baffled me.

There was a basic confusion going on, I wanted to explain. I'd only arrived a few minutes before, an hour at the most. I tried to find words to make her understand, but then I noticed that she wasn't the same woman as before. No, she was the same woman, but now she wore a pink tank top with CK printed on the front instead of the Monet shirt. Her silver hair no longer hung down around her shoulders, but was now piled high on her head. Why would she change clothes and hair like this? Why would she try to trick me? What had I ever done to her? I gave her money so that I could go away, back to my room to rest. If I could only get some sleep, everything would be okay, everything would start to make sense again. I hobbled up the stairs and into my room. I closed the door against the rest of the world—all of it but the music—drank a mouthful of water, put the banana on the night stand and fell onto the bed.

I didn't sleep, but I felt comfortable with my eyes closed and my body pulsing and shimmering and warm. If only they'd turn the music off, I'd be fine. As it was, I would have to leave this hotel, just as soon as I rested up a bit. I sank down into a gray-blue void like warm, deep water, floated until that sharp stabbing in my stomach brought me up and out, back into the room and thumping music. I climbed out of bed, stumbled to the bathroom, and down the stairs. By the time I reached the lobby, I knew I'd never have the strength to escape this place.

"*¡Gringo!*" The woman at the desk shouted, just as she'd shouted a dozen, a hundred times before. This meant that it was time to give her money. I walked over but didn't look at her face. I put bills on the counter, and a bleach-white hand slide across the worn wood and clutched them. I glanced up and saw pink lips, white cheeks and chin pocked with red sores. I didn't need to see the pale dreadlocks to recognize the *gringa* photographer who'd wanted to capture me falling to my death from the temple at Tikal. If I could only get some sleep, I could escape. But now I had to climb up the stairs, back to room eleven.

I woke in pain, curled like a pill bug until the cramp passed. Then I rolled out of bed and hustled to the bathroom. When I returned to the room, I saw my backpack unopened on the floor, a black banana and a nearly-empty gallon jug of water on the night stand, and a brownish stain on the otherwise smooth bed sheet. I tried to count the times I'd paid the woman at the desk, how many nights I'd spent here. I came up with six, a rough estimate. My boots felt as if they were filled with warm jelly. The music was so loud the water jug trembled. My guts were a mess, but my mind was back.

That evening, safely checked into a perfectly quiet hotel up by the highway, I decided to try to eat something. I made my way to the open-air market, and took a seat at a beans and rice eatery tucked in among the produce stands. A dark-skinned woman cooked at a long table set up with gas stoves. A boy served the four tables. I ordered a Coke and tried to read the stained menu.

"Congratulations," the only other customer said, a lean man in a beret, perhaps sixty years old. He spoke English with a Latino accent, but he spoke it comfortably. "You found the best food in Tela. Where are you from, friend? You look tired."

"The United States," I said.

"I would have guessed. You Yankees, no offense, stand out. I'm from Argentina, but I don't consider Argentina home anymore. Now I'm from everywhere. In the summer, I seek the sun. In the winter, I go to the snow. Crazy? Yes. I think so. But snow is good for painting. You can't paint in this heat, so I don't try."

He paused to sip coffee, and I thought that was the end of his story.

"When I was younger," he continued, "I'd try to paint in summer. I thought I had to paint all the time or I was no painter. Now I don't care if I'm a real painter or not. What's the difference? In the summer, I eat, drink, sit in the shade and watch the beautiful women pass."

The boy brought my Coke. I drank through the straw, belched, and finished it off in a few gulps. I wanted only a plate of rice but despaired of explaining this to the boy. These little places always seemed to take offence when you ordered off the menu. I asked for the egg dish and another Coke.

"How about you?" the painter asked. "What brings you to paradise?"

"I almost died," I said, surprised at my own words.

"Oh? You didn't come here for that, did you?"

"I slept for a whole week. I didn't know what was happening. Nobody knows I'm here. I'd have slipped away without even realizing it."

"Malaria," the painter said, and for some reason a flush of satisfaction spread through me, and some tightness in my chest I hadn't been aware of loosened. It confused me, this reaction, and I put it out of my mind.

The boy delivered the Coke and food. The dish came with bacon, and the smell made me queasy. I tried to eat a forkful of rice, but my hand shook so badly the rice kept falling back onto my plate. I dropped the fork and shoveled some rice into my mouth with my fingers. It was good.

"Adios," the artist said. "Take care of yourself, young man."

"Adios," I replied, and I realized I'd felt this surprised sense of well being before, back when my father had first told me about the murder, and my reaction had been wonder and pride, pride in having brushed so closely with something so big and powerful as that, as death. And now here I was, a grown man, chronologically at least, just as proud to have caught malaria, as if that were some kind of achievement and not just evidence of folly. But I couldn't help it. I felt better than I had in months, so I quit worrying why.

The diarrhea lasted another ten days, and then I felt more or less myself, just a little weak. Shopping for lunch in the market, I ran my thumb over an avocado's skin, squeezed it lightly. "I know you," came a voice from behind. I turned to face a sleepy-eyed guy I recognized but couldn't place. His yellow hair hung straight down over his forehead and ears, and he wore safari pants and a polo shirt over his slim body.

"Steve," I said. I'd met him my first days in Guatemala, during one of my weekend excursions while studying. "Panajachel, right?"

"That's it. Seems ages. Hey, you have plans for dinner? I'm getting sick of beans and rice, so I thought I'd buy something fresh, cook it over a fire on the beach. Interested?"

I said I was, and we set out to shop: limes, onions, garlic, potatoes, mangos, cilantro…not really thinking, just grabbing whatever looked good. Steve bought a thick roll of banana leaves, explaining that locals used them as plates.

We took our groceries to the beach, sat in the sand to wait for the fisherman to return. A little later, Steve recognized another friend from the road who happened to be walking by. His name was Aaron, a homely, freckled man with a patchy beard, wearing a University of Oregon baseball cap. We invited him to join us. "Sure," he said, "as long as it's cheap. I'm almost out of money."

"Best deal in town," Steve assured him, and Aaron sat down in the sand with us. The fishermen returned later that afternoon, driving their *lanchas* up onto the damp sand. We waited until the restaurant owners and local home cooks made their purchases, and then haggled for a red snapper nearly two feet long and a bag of live blue crabs.

Loaded with plastic grocery bags and Steve's daypack full of camp cookware, we walked down the beach away from town. Restaurants and hotels gave way to a dense bamboo forest that rose like a fence a hundred yards from shore. Seaweed and shabby twists of driftwood etched gentle arcs along the high water line, and vultures with oily-looking feathers and pink heads watched us pass, now and then spearing the sand with their beaks or shaking their wings as if settling into coats. "I'll take a seagull over one of those guys any day," I said.

"I think they're kind of cute," Aaron put in. One of the vultures stood in front of us and raised its wings to the breeze like a preacher filled with The Spirit. We gave it a wide berth.

About a mile from town, we dropped our bags in the sand and radiated out to collect driftwood and dead bamboo for a fire. Soon a large pile lay beside the bags. Aaron began to break down the bigger branches, sometimes propping one against a thick log nearby and performing an elaborate kick, calling out "hi-yah!" He made sure to stomp on each airtight section of bamboo to break the sealed chamber before tossing it into the firewood pile. Steve, meanwhile, removed a machete from his backpack and carried it off to a cluster of palms near the bamboo. With my hands, I dug a pit for the fire and ringed it with stones. I built an elaborate pyre, beginning with slivers of kindling and progressing to the heaviest pieces. Steve returned and dropped six fresh coconuts into the sand near the groceries.

Vultures gathered a dozen feet away, where the gray water raked the shore with a sound like labored breath. The sun, a blurry white hole in the beige sky, hung just above the point where land met water in the western distance, this being a north-facing shore. I opened a book of matches. "It's so pretty you almost don't want to burn it," Aaron said, as I lit the kindling. The fire leapt up so quickly we had to hurry to move the plastic bags so they wouldn't melt. The dry wood burned down in no time, and we piled more onto the shallow bed of coals.

"Look," Steve whispered. A dozen little kids stood watching us from thirty yards away, black boys and girls known as Garifuna, descendants of shipwrecked slaves from various parts of Africa who'd settled these parts, forming a unique language and culture. Behind them, several mangy dogs sat on their haunches.

"What do they want?" Aaron asked.

"Nothing," Steve said. "They're just not used to seeing gringos this far from town."

"They're creeping me out a little," I said.

Steve turned his back to the kids and stared at the fire. "They won't do anything."

I carried the snapper down to the water, and pulled the Swiss Army knife from the wax pocket of my trunks. My father had always traveled with a knife like this one, and I could picture it slicing an apple in two, half for me, half for him, washed down with cool water from his army-surplus canteen. The image was a specific one, a bit of memory from the time he'd taught me to hitchhike, from Anza to the beach.

I laid the fish on the damp sand and slit the belly. I'd only been fishing once, on a lake with Ralph, and at the end of the day, Ralph had showed me how to gut and clean the half-dozen bluegills we'd caught. I used the same technique now, but instead of a hose I cleaned the fish in the sea. Back at the fire, I cut the strand of banana leaf fiber that secured the roll, and the leaves unfurled, dark green and firm in the grocery sack. I placed several of them overlapping on the sand, forming a cooking station of sorts. I scored the pinkish-white sides of the snapper with deep slashes, salted and peppered it inside and out. I then sliced lime, onion, and garlic, and yanked the top off the bundle of cilantro. All of this went into the cavity of the fish. Then I wrapped the whole thing in a banana leaf and tied it off with a string of fiber. I wasn't sure where I'd learned to do this, perhaps a cooking show on cable or just some innate, or maybe ancestral knowledge.

Meanwhile, the fire had burned down to a thick bed of coals. Into this, Steve tossed several small, round potatoes. "My dad used to cook them this way when we camped," he mused, and I imagined my father seeing me now, and thought that he'd be impressed.

Steve filled a pot with seawater and balanced it over a hot spot of coals on three stones. "For the crabs," he said, sliding wood under the pot to build a hot flame. "Poor bastards."

I took up one of the green *cocos* and slid the knife's blade into the top, surprised at how easily it cut through the dense, moist husk. A little sawing motion around the stem and a circular cap came out like a cork. I passed the coco to Aaron while Steve opened his own with a couple of whacks from the machete. I prepared a third coco for myself, while Aaron produced a bottle of dark rum. "Here's the secret ingredient," he said, pouring some into his coconut. He passed the bottle to Steve, who then passed it to me. I hesitated for a moment—I hadn't taken any alcohol since I'd gotten sick—before splashing a shot into my coco.

Steve, one of those resourceful people, handed out straws. When the water began to boil, Aaron dumped in the crabs, and pushed them down with a stick. A few seconds later they were still. I placed the fish packet onto a clear space in the coals, and already the crabs and potatoes gave off a wonderful smell. The vultures and dogs remained, but the children had gone.

The sun was setting as we spread the feast over a fresh blanket of banana leaves. Pleasantly famished and high on rum, we dove in with our hands. I popped a hearty flake of snapper into my mouth and allowed the moist, tart and sweet flesh to dissolve on my tongue. Next I went after a crab, pulling it apart with my hands and sucking out the meat. Juice dripped down my chin and I stripped off my shirt. Steve did the same and then Aaron. I squeezed several more limes over the whole spread, and we snatched up the food by the fistful. We used coconut bread rolls and the creamy potatoes to mop up the juices. When the snapper had been reduced to a skeleton on one side, I flipped it and we dove in for more. We ate down to bones, shells, peels, and a sheen of oil. I sucked out the rest of my coco water and rum, and then split the husk in two to get at the jellied flesh.

The sun had gone, and the sky above the horizon glowed the same orange as the coal pit. "Dessert?" I asked, and tossed a mango to each of the guys. We peeled them with our fingers and teeth, ate the meat, and sucked the pits. We rolled the remains of our feast into the banana leaves and flung them to the dogs and vultures, which fell to, squabbling and jostling.

Sticky with fish and mango, we walked to the water. I waded out to my chest. Aaron and Steve stripped to boxers and joined me. I ducked under and scrubbed. I filled my lungs and floated face down as long as I could stand it. Back at the fire, shivering slightly in the cooling evening, we opened new coconuts, added more rum, and sat in easy silence.

"Splitting this coconut," Steve said to me, the first words spoken in some time, "reminds me of something strange that happened just before I met you in Panajachel. I went to one of those full moon parties they have across the lake in San Pedro, kind of a hippy thing. Me and this guy I just met started off with a bunch of pot cookies. The high was really coming on, bonfire, drums, the whole deal. Everyone drinking wine and passing joints. I figured I'd go with it, started dancing around, getting weird. Earlier that day, I found this two-headed pineapple in the market. I thought it was cool, so I brought it to the party."

"I know this story," I said.

Steve paused, face orange and eyes lit a demonic orange. "Yeah?"

"You sliced the pineapple down the middle and your friend, named Walter, got scared and ran off."

Steve threw a log on the coals. A lacy flame sprang to life and began to crawl over it. "How'd you know?" he asked.

"I know more than that," I said, and told him the rest.

"I'm broke," Aaron said, apropos of nothing.

"I met Walter a few weeks ago," I admitted. "Nothing psychic or anything. He told me the story. You know, he thinks you meant to sacrifice him."

"I don't want to go home," Aaron said. "But I'm out of money. What can I do?"

"What are the odds?" Steve asked. "I mean, of us even meeting here and making this food, much less you knowing about Walter and the pineapple."

"Listen to me for a minute," Aaron said. "I'm asking for advice. I hear that if you go broke in Honduras the U.S. consulate will buy you a ticket home. You know anything about that?"

The lone flame had dug into the log in two intersecting veins. I shoved it deeper into the coals with a poker stick, fascinated by the fire's persistence. "Sounds reasonable to me," I said.

"Yeah," Steve agreed, "they wouldn't let you run out of money and die over here, would they? I mean, you're an American."

"I think you're right," Aaron said. "I should do it. I'll hang around until the money is gone, and show up on their doorstep. Maybe I'll pretend I was robbed."

"But what if they don't care?" I posited. "I've seen homeless Americans down here. Well, white people at least. Wandering around just like the homeless back home."

"Homeless back home," Aaron repeated.

"Here's another question," I said, unable to break my gaze from the fire. "Steve asked about odds." I paused to consider precisely what I wanted to express. "But what are the odds of us being here at all? Being foreigners in Central America? Being humans instead of vultures? Of being here on this planet instead of some other? Sitting at this particular fire, talking about this very thing? Of existing at all?"

"Astronomical," Aaron said, spreading his arms to encompass the slate sky. The line of gold along the western horizon was as thin as thread, and no moon had risen. The coals' orange glow lit Steve and Aaron's necks as they stared skyward at the pale wash of stars above. A plane traveled slowly across the firmament, but otherwise I saw the sky as the ancients must have, as a dark and spangled ceiling hemming us in. But then it changed. As I stared, the fire warming my bare legs and chest, I apprehended the infinity of space, all that darkness containing uncountable spheres, each whirling and circling, in concert. I sensed the

Earth moving, both the spin and the orbit; for a second, I got it, all of it coming together, a feeling that transcended words, and then a sharp crack rang out like a gunshot, and a spray of fire flew at my face and body. I threw my arms over my eyes and squirmed away from the tiny burns, hands everywhere brushing at the little bits of fire. Around us, twenty feet out in a perfect circle, hundreds of pinpoint orange lights pulsed, our own little constellation blanketing the waves of black sand.

"Bamboo," Aaron said after a moment, his voice as thin as the breeze riffling our hair. "A section of bamboo I forgot to break. It exploded." His voice had picked up momentum, took on a mild authority. "That's all."

"Yeah, but still," I said, and left it at that, while all around us the tiny orange lights pulsed, shivered, and blinked out, ember by ember.

Chapter Seven

Haight Street

I pushed the buzzer on the security gate between the Pork Store Cafe and Anarchist Books. My old friend Brett lived in the apartment upstairs. He used to at least. I hadn't seen him in ages. Up the street, an electrical bus came loose from the overhead wires, leaving it stalled in traffic, its duel antennae spinning and bouncing foolishly. Signs along the street exclaimed this and that: Zam Zam, Abba Dabba, Puff Puff Pass. Cars honked. Pedestrians scrambled, jaywalking, passing each other, going and coming through doorways. I'd forgotten how fast everything happened in San Francisco. For all its simmering violence, Central America moved at a languid pace, and all this first-world rushing about gave me the jimjams.

"Spare a buck for a vegi burrito, brother?" The question came from a dirty kid huddled with a girl and a puppy in the doorway of the bookstore.

"Not today," I said, implying that I might feel differently tomorrow.

"It's all good," he replied, another lie. I imagined this pair had escaped some suburb or other, chasing the endless acid trip carnival that was the Grateful Dead on tour. I could understand the attraction of such a venture, the urge to escape the tedium of a basic American existence, and I held a grudging respect for these self-appointed refugees, but I didn't appreciate their style.

Not a moment too soon, the door upstairs opened, rescuing me from the guilt trip beaming up from the young hippies and their whimpering dog.

"No way!" Brett said, unlocking the gate. "You just fly in? I thought I'd never see you again."

"Well, yeah," I replied. "I landed a couple hours ago. Listen. I hate to put you on the spot, but you mind letting me crash for a night?" I gestured to the Marrakesh to show my circumstances.

"Hell yes. One night? Stay for a week. Actually, you can move in. I'm about to post an ad for a roommate. Come on up."

I'd never imagined living on Haight Street, but why not? "If you're serious about the room," I said, propping my bag in the hall, "I'm your man. Maybe. But first, you mind if I make a long-distance call? I'm good for the charges."

"Of course." Brett was twenty-five years old, with a long narrow jaw, fine blond hair and a little dark soul patch under his lip. His hair had receded a bit since I'd last seen him, and his middle had filled out, but otherwise he still had that lanky, slightly clumsy, affable quality that made him easy to like.

He showed me to the front bedroom, the one for rent, empty except for a phone on the stained carpet. It was a good-sized space, with three windows overlooking the street, just above the Pork Store's jutting sign. Brett closed the door, and I dialed my grandmother, pacing with the phone in hand. "Good Lord!" she said. "I didn't know if you were dead or alive down there. I thought you liked to write."

"Didn't you get my letter?"

"That was months ago."

"Months? Well, I'm sorry—"

"Your father's been given six years," she said. "With time served and good behavior, he'll be out in less than two."

I stopped pacing and stood there, staring at a large nail hole. My father's trial had been dragging on for a year, and I'd figured the defense was just stalling, putting off the inevitable. "Really?" I finally said.

"I wanted to tell you sooner, but I had no way to reach you."

"I'm sorry," I repeated, struggling to adjust to the new situation. In my mind, ten years had seemed overly optimistic. Twenty was reasonable, and I was prepared for life. I should have felt elated, but I was just confused, and something akin to irritated.

"Every day," Helen explained, "I put on my best clothes and went to court. Our lawyer told me it was important for the jury to see that the defendant came from a good family. Gil went when he could; you know how busy he is. But I never missed a day. It wasn't easy, but it had to be done."

"I don't get it," I muttered, but what was there, really, to get? What I meant was that it didn't seem right. I hadn't wanted my father to spend most his remaining years in prison—far from it—but I'd felt, basically, that he probably deserved to. He'd shot a man, killed him forever, and then he'd run away, leaving his parents to forfeit bail. Pot dealers got stiffer sentences than six years.

Helen went on about the trial, speaking of manslaughter versus murder one, a cocky, overreaching prosecutor and the best defense in Orange County; private investigators, lost evidence, reluctant, dead, or disappeared witnesses. The dog Dad had rescued in Anza, a husky that had shown up outside the cabin with one of its front legs blown off, had played into the favorable verdict. Even Barkley's son, supposedly stalking me all these years, had issued a statement on behalf of the defense. I felt like a fool.

Helen followed the good news with an update on my brother. He'd gotten busted in a trailer full of meth cooking equipment, chemicals, and weapons. He hadn't been sentenced yet, but the odds weren't in his favor. So there it was. My grandparents' money would get Dad off easy, but no soft landing for Ole. Gil was rich by my standards, but not two generations worth of rich. They'd spent their lives earning it, and Dad spent his blowing through it.

I hung up the phone but didn't leave the room right away. Across the street, a makeshift band had started jamming, a guitar and a couple of hand drums. The guitarist, a blond Swede with a red, alcoholic face, vaguely resembled my uncle Gerick. He'd been around a lot after my dad and mom divorced, and I'd both loved and loathed him.

"So," Brett said, back in the living room, "what's happening? How was the trip?"

I looked around the typical San Francisco flat living room, at the dusty television, windows with a view of the fire escape next door, furniture left by roommates long past. For whatever reason, I couldn't think of anything to say about Central America. I felt shy, tongue-tied. I hadn't been around an actual friend for a long time. "You know how Rachel's doing?" I finally asked.

Brett shook his head and shrugged. "Last I heard, she moved back to L.A. I think she's got a boyfriend down there. That's about it. I'm sure she's over whatever went down between the two of you by now. Life goes on."

"I didn't handle the breakup very well."

"Don't beat yourself up. It's done. So what do you think about the room? You get used to the noise. It fades into the background. Like listening to the ocean as you sleep. The great sea of humanity."

"I'll take it. All I need is a futon."

"That and a job," Brett added.

◆

Six months later, I entered the kitchen and found Brett writing on the chalkboard where we divvied up the bills. He stood to the side to show me.

RIP Jerry Garcia

8-9-95

"Okay," I said, rummaging through the cupboard for coffee filters. "Bummer for him."

"I'm not a big fan of the Dead either," Brett said, "but think about where we are. Right in the middle of history."

I pictured the scruffy orphans on the sidewalk, and realized Brett was right. We happened to be in the epicenter of all things Grateful Dead, and the hippies would come to mourn their fallen father. "And you know what else?" I said. "We're out of coffee filters."

The band's last show had been on the east coast, so it took several days for the brokenhearted followers to show up in mass, setting up vigils on corners and doorways, lighting candles, chalking concrete, smoking dope, spare changing, and wandering about like the lost children they were. The day before a big memorial concert in the park, Brett and I set up chairs at my windows and sat with a six pack on ice to watch the spectacle. "I just heard a new one," Brett said. "How can you tell a Deadhead's been to your place?"

"I don't know. How?"

"He's still there."

The Swedish guitar player was still there too, at his usual spot across the street in front of the liquor store. His group was involved in some kind of dispute with a rival bunch, newly arrived and camped out a few feet down the sidewalk. They'd been drunkenly squabbling all afternoon, and it made for good entertainment.

"I set out for Reno, I was trailed by twenty hounds," I sang, and Brett joined in. "Couldn't get to sleep last night til morning came around."

"Set out running but I take my time, a friend of the devil is a friend of mine. If I get home before daylight, I just might get some sleep, to-ni-hite."

"There it is," Brett said, "the only Dead lyrics I know."

"Same here. My dad used to play that song for me when I was a little kid."

"My folks went in for 'Twinkle, Twinkle Little Star.'"

"I loved 'Friend of the Devil', even though it freaked me out."

"Probably why you loved it."

"Friend of the Devil. Think about it. What a weird concept. I mean, when you're a kid, you think grownups have all the answers. God is good. Bad people are punished. David kills Goliath. You trust that there's some order in the universe, some justice. But listening to that song must have been one of my first clues that it wasn't really like that."

"What's the part about the guy having two wives? One of them has my child but he don't look like me?"

"I used to wonder why, and how, the dead could be grateful. It felt like all the adults were keeping some secret from me, and I really needed to find out what it was."

"Drugs," Brett said, and popped the cap from a beer. "That's what you were missing. Sex with someone you're not supposed to have sex with. All those things that feel good but aren't good for you, which is like, everything. That's what the Devil is. He's a metaphor for temptation."

"It's all Eve's fault, right?"

At this point, the Swede set his guitar on the ground and jumped up angrily. He stood face-to-face with the leader of the opposing group, a big guy who bore a passing resemblance to his recently departed hero.

"How's your dad doing, anyway? Isn't he getting out soon?"

"About a year. My grandmother's been on me to move back to Laguna, to be around when he's set free."

"Nothing wrong with that. You going to take her up on it?"

"Maybe, if Mexico doesn't work out."

Brett was about to fly to Istanbul, to put to use his newly-minted certificate in Teaching English as a Second Language. I intended to follow in his footsteps, after my own, informal fashion, by crossing into Mexico and looking around for teaching gigs. To this end, I'd volunteered with Brett once, giving a free English lesson to immigrants in the Mission. I figured to print up a resume that exaggerated this fifteen-minute lesson into actual teaching experience. I hoped that this plus a bachelor's degree would be enough paper to score me a job.

"Plus," I admitted, "I'm curious about him. Last we really talked, besides the time I visited him in jail or spoke on the phone, I was a little kid. He'd been kind of a kid, too, now that I think about it. Imagine having a baby at eighteen."

"Well, there they go," Brett said. "Bound to happen I guess."

The Swede was rolling on the ground with the Jerry Garcia look-alike. A dozen others stood around, shouting. Nobody seemed interested in breaking them up, and neither was fit enough to inflict any real damage.

"I ever tell you that blond one looks like my uncle?" I asked.

The Swede had gained the upper hand, and sat on top of Garcia, though neither was able to land a punch.

"Uncle Gerick lived with us out in the desert when I was a kid. Back then, I thought he was the coolest. He'd take us on long hikes, help us build forts, and racetracks and jumps for our bikes. And he'd tell the craziest stories. I mean, nutty stuff that sounds stupid now, but then… Like once we hiked up into the mountains to a huge, fallen tree out in the forest, a cedar I think, and he convinced us, me, my brother and his four boys, that it was a crashed UFO. I was like nine, and I didn't doubt him for a second. I still remember running along that tree, the size of a small jet I guess, totally lost in this spacey dream world. It was like acid, but without the fear or the unreality. The kind of thing dopers are always looking for but never find. It always seemed to be like that with Gerick.

"This other time he drove me around a really nice suburban neighborhood, about twilight. I don't remember what we were doing there, or why I was alone with him. I just remember him driving very slowly, pointing out the people walking their dogs, a couple eating dinner in a big window, framed like they were posing just for us, two long candles on the table. Just a normal night, but again the feeling I'd had with the fallen tree. It was like Gerick could cast a spell. At that moment, everything looked a little too perfect to be real, the lawns, the sidewalks, flower beds, mailboxes. I guess I'd never seen a neighborhood quite like that before, wealthy but not crazy rich. Then Gerick told me, quiet, like this was a big secret I had to keep, that all the people we saw walking around or sitting in their houses were robots, put there by the government."

Brett laughed, and so did I. "Was he joking?"

"To this day, I don' know. But it made perfect sense at the time. Maybe he was talking in metaphors, or just screwing with me. He could have believed it, for all I know. Especially considering what he eventually became. But anyway, it was always like that when I hung out with him, some mind-blowing revelation. Too bad it was all bullshit."

"Doesn't sound terrible, as far as lies go," Brett said. "What's the difference between government robot conspiracies, and Santa and the Easter Bunny? What's he doing now?"

"He's dead. Lit himself on fire and burned up."

"Damn. On purpose?"

"No. Accident. He lived on one of those desert properties full of junked cars, trailers, shacks, and a bunch of homemade tents. He'd lost it by then, lived with a crazy alcoholic woman and a bunch of their kids. One cold night, he got drunk and decided to bed down in a tent. It was made of nylon, and heated with a jerry-rigged propane heater. The cops figure the fuel line must have slipped, ignited and started spraying fire all through the tent, like a flame thrower. The melted nylon fell onto him, stuck there, and he walked a hundred yards on fire, to a neighbor's house. They got him to a hospital, but it was too late. He died a few days later, bloated up twice his size."

"Jesus."

"They had to make these two big cuts down his sides," I said, "from armpit to thigh, so the fluid could drain. Below the bed they set big metal pans to catch the gunk."

"That's just awful."

"Yeah, well, I don't know if he deserved to die like that, but he deserved something. He was full crazy by that time. After he and my aunt divorced, he took two of their four sons. When I knew him, he could be pretty brutal, especially to his own boys. He didn't mess with me much, except to make fun of me when I complained or whatever. His big thing was he didn't want us to turn into 'sissies,' so he teased us and smacked us around a good bit, and we weren't allowed to cry or whine. In one way, it wasn't the worst lesson to learn, but he eventually turned into a full-on child abuser. The kind of stuff you read about. Even weirder, he decided he was some kind of holy man, and he'd hold these religious services on his property, mostly for his own kids I guess, maybe a few of the wacky people that lived around there. Once he had the boys bury his young daughter in a box, so he could dig her up during the service. Something about resurrection. Finally they arrested him for molesting his girls."

"Oh, man."

"No kidding. I still can't believe I looked up to a guy like that. You know, he taught me how to ride a bike. Stood there on my third birthday for hours and forced me to do it, even though I was crying and scraped up and hating him. But then I started riding, and the hatred just kind of blew off me."

"You got off pretty easy, compared to his other kids, especially the ones he molested," Brett pointed out.

"Yes. I was lucky. I hear all the kids he had with the alcoholic are in trouble. One boy for rape. Others locked up o r in rehab. Dude left a big mess behind."

A cop car pulled up to the fight, and two officers waded in. Everybody was clamoring to tell their side of the story, and one of the officers stood there rubbing his temples like he was oh-so tired of these people.

"I got two reasons why I cry away each lonely night," I sang, softly this time. "The first one is la-la, la-la; la-la, la-la-la-la-la-la. The second one is prison, babe, the sheriff's on my trail. And if he catches up to me, I'll spend my life in jail."

Brett chuckled. "That sheriff," he said, as the Swede was helped into the back of the squad car, "he always catches up to you eventually."

"Maybe so," I said, thinking of O.J. Simpson, on trial and surely about to do hard time, if not worse. Maybe we all got what we deserved in the end.

Chapter Eight

Puerto Vallarta

Hoping to get a feel for the place, meet a local or two, I loafed along the boardwalk, where trinket salesmen hawked their wares over the competing racket of three discos across the highway. I'd arrived the day before and thought I might like to stay. "Paint your name on a grain of rice?" called a short guy with a bowl haircut. The sign above his head stated these exact words. I was about to wave him off when I noticed his tee shirt, white with black letters advertising "The USA School." I'd seen these shirts all over town.

"Do you mind turning around?" I asked. He frowned until I made a whirling motion with my finger. Across the back ran an italicized sentence wrapped in quotation marks.

"*'I've always found that you must work for everything you gain in life'* – José Luis Santana, Owner, USA School."

"Is this an English school?" I asked. Just that morning, I'd checked a phone book for language schools, and the only one listed had led to an empty building.

"Sí," he replied, a little sullen now that he saw I wasn't going to pay him to paint my name on a grain of rice. "I graduated from Level One," he boasted in Spanish. "Next week I start Level Two."

I asked for the address and he gave me a street name, pointing north toward Nuevo Vallarta, several miles of sky-rise resorts that hugged the shore outside of town.

"Far?"

"No. A few blocks."

I thanked him and walked the rest of the way up the boardwalk, where I hopped down and hustled across the busy highway. At the next corner I accidentally caught the eye of a lanky teenager manning one of the bright white kiosks scattered all over town. I didn't know the function these uniformed kids served, but they were everywhere, accosting passersby with glossy photos of vacation splendor, yachts and jet skis and beautiful women lounging on sugar-sand beaches. Whatever they were selling, I couldn't afford. "Hey dude," said the youth, "you want to make a hundred pesos?"

I stopped. "Hundred pesos?" That was somewhere around ten bucks. I knew it must be a scam, but I was curious. No such thing as a free lunch! Solter shouted in my head, but I chose not to listen.

"Come here," the kid said, looking left and right to be sure the coast was clear. "I ain't gonna bite you. My name's Rudy." He stuck out his hand, and I accepted it reluctantly. "I look at you and say, this guy doesn't want to buy a timeshare. You got those sandals, that shirt. So I'm not going to waste your time with a pitch. Here's the truth. Every time I sign somebody up for a presentation, they pay me two hundred pesos. I'll split it with you, bro. A hundred pesos, and all you have to do is eat breakfast and see a hotel room. It takes about a hour. Easy money. Hundred for you, hundred for me. No problem."

I thought for a moment. A hundred pesos would pay for my hotel room that night—nothing to retire on but it was a start. And I'd be grifting the grifters, sticking it to the big chain hotels that were taking over the world and sapping the last bit of authenticity from towns like Vallarta. "Okay," I said. "How often can I do it?"

"How often?" Rudy covered his surprise, and I felt a stab of misgiving.

"You can do it every day if you want."

"What about twice a day?" I calculated that I could live on that, especially with a couple of free meals thrown in.

"No problem. Let me set something up for tomorrow to start."

"When do I get paid?"

"Call me when you're done, and I'll pick you up."

"No way."

"Okay, fifty when I drop you off, fifty when I pick you up. I can't steal your money, dude. I work here every day."

"Deal," I said. How bad could it be?

Early the next morning, Rudy took me by taxi to the Mayan Palace Resort. I walked through a crowd of old folks in cabana wear, by a fountain shaped like a Mayan pyramid spewing water from its tip. In the echoing lobby, I shook a skinny, wrinkled man's hand. He wore a suit but smelled strongly of cigarette smoke and his fly was half down. "Dick," he said, pumping my hand, "Dick Rueben." He pointed me to the "deluxe breakfast buffet," where I ate chafing-dish fare and drank watery coffee. Stuffed and jittery, I was led to a small, windowless office and sat across a desk from Dick. Now in private, he sighed theatrically. Of all the rotten luck, he was thinking, looking me over with a little shake of his head, I get a guy in a stained tee shirt who hasn't shaved in a week. I'd dressed raggedly in *huarache* sandals and canvas shorts, thinking they'd let me go early if I gave them no hope of a sale.

"I'm not going to buy anything," I announced. "You might as well turn me loose and save the trouble."

"It's not so easy, friend," he said, and opened a photo album full of the sorts of pictures that lined the kiosks. "We're stuck with each other." He smiled, showing brown teeth, sadism firing his beady black eyes. And then he was off, interrogating me. How often do you vacation? I never vacation. What do you call what you're doing now? Living. Okay, how often do you live? I don't understand the question.

On and on it went, Dick asking questions from an endless stack of forms, me more-or-less answering truthfully. Just an hour, I thought, and went into robot mode. But an hour turned into an hour and a half, and then two hours, and we'd only gotten through half the papers on Dick's desk. The walls were bare white, and Dick's only decoration was a framed picture on his desk of several interlocking gears and "SYNERGY" written below in yellow print. "Shouldn't we be done by now?" I asked.

"We'll get you out of here soon," Dick said, smiling evilly. Numbers played a big part in the argument. He'd push graphs and charts at me, explaining how this plus this equaled I'd be the biggest dipshit in history if I didn't sign his papers. I could no longer even try to make sense of what he was saying. I just heard the monotone of his voice, watching his ever-moving, hangdog mouth surrounded by black stubble. A waddle swung below his chin as he talked. "How about some fresh air?" he finally asked, going on three hours.

"Thank you," I said, vaguely aware that I was succumbing to Stockholm syndrome.

We walked out of the main building, onto a dock in a manmade bay. Dick produced a key and led me into a bungalow on the dock. It was a serviceable room with a view of a beach fenced off even out into the water. "Shark-free swimming," Dick said, following my gaze. "Kick off your shoes. Try the bed."

I touched the mattress. It was covered in a slick-feeling spread decorated with red and yellow boxes. The room smelled of some kind of sweet air freshener, a chemical version of strawberry, I decided. "No thanks," I said. "I'll fall asleep and then you'll just wake me up. Actually, I'm pretty ready to leave."

"Don't worry. We're almost done."

"I've heard that before," I said, my voice about to crack. "I'm five seconds from walking out."

"What about your gift?" he asked. "Do you want to forfeit the commemorative tequila or traditional blanket when you're so close?"

I sighed and stared out the window at the people on the beach, free to come and go as they pleased.

"Come on," he said. "Cheer up. I'll introduce you to Jim. Jim's a great guy. He used to play for the Dallas Cowboys. What do you think of that?"

"I think it's sad," I said, and we walked back into the hotel.

Dick knocked on a hollow, walnut-paneled door. "Come in," called a deep voice. The man standing behind the desk was large and meaty, with an enormous belly and jowls tinged red. An inch of gray roots gave way to a head of Clairol-brown hair over a perfectly square face. He gripped my hand as I knew he would, one degree tighter than firm. My own hand was sweaty, and I was trembling from fatigue and coffee comedown. Dick left us, and I sat. Jim's office was twice the size of Dick's and looked out on a parking lot. Two of the four walls were covered in Dallas Cowboy banners, posters, and trinkets; the remaining wall space was devoted to sports-themed motivational posters, including a giant one of Vince Lombardi which apparently included the entire text of his most famous speech.

"Dick treat you right?"

I shrugged, thinking, no, he badgered me for three and a half hours, but I had no desire to complain to this man, who I already liked less than even the odious Dick. "I see you looking at my ring," Jim said, smiling. In contrast to Dick's stained teeth, Jim's were whiter than was natural, and large. He held out his right hand as if I were expected to kiss the giant ring. Among diamonds, I read the words "Dallas Cowboys World Champions."

"Nice," I said. "I take it you were on the team?"

"That's the only way to get one of these babies."

"What'd you play?"

"Linebacker. Special teams."

"You look it," I said.

"Thanks. Now let's get to business." His smile collapsed as he shuffled through the papers before him. When he looked up, he appeared angry. "I see you're single?"

"Yes."

"You mean to meet a woman someday?"

"I meet women all the time."

"I'm talking about a good woman. A woman to marry."

"I'm not looking for a wife, no."

"Are you a faggot?"

I opened my mouth to respond, but couldn't find anything to say.

"Just kidding," Jim said. "No, but seriously. Are you homosexual?"

"No," I said. "Do I look gay?" It was a stupid question, and I immediately regretted asking it.

Jim didn't respond. "My point is," he said, "that you've got to grow up one day. You're pushing thirty and, one, you don't have a job, two, you don't have a pot to piss in, three, you look like a vagabond. I wouldn't be surprised if that's where you end up if you keep on this road, in the streets, begging for food and hooch. You need to learn to take responsibility, to accept the commitments that separate men from boys. Personally, I think buying one of our properties, joining our little family, would be a perfect start for a guy like you. For just a few bucks a month, you'll actually own something. Think of that. Imagine meeting a woman, a real quality lady. Think what she'll say when you tell her that you don't just have one vacation home, you've got hundreds. How many guys can say that?"

"Listen," I said, "I told Dick a hundred times—"

"You leave Dick out of this!" Jim shouted.

I leaned far back in my chair. It seemed possible he'd attack me.

"You're talking to me now. Forget everything else."

"I'm leaving," I announced.

"Hey, hey." Jim was up and blocking the door. "Come on, buddy, don't be so sensitive. You don't want to miss out on the gift, do you? Not after all this work we've put in. We're almost there."

"That's what everybody keeps telling me," I said, tears pushing at my eyelids, "but it just doesn't end."

"Come on. Sit down. Don't be a baby."

Now Jim was wounded. After all he and the others had done for me, I was still refusing to be "a part of the family." I rolled my head back and looked at the dropped-tile ceiling, just like the ones back in the States. I answered in monosyllables and shrugged a lot. Finally, after forty minutes with Jim, the pitch was over. Jim, disappointed, hurt, and angry, led me to a secretary, who had me sign a form that confirmed I'd elected not to buy a timeshare in spite of everyone's best efforts, and then she asked if I wanted a blanket or tequila.

"Tequila."

"I knew you'd say that." She handed me a miniscule cardboard box, allegedly containing a bottle.

From a pay phone outside, I dialed the number Rudy had given me, and ten minutes later he picked me up in the same cab that had dropped me off. "Here you go," he said, and handed me a fifty peso bill. "I got another presentation arranged for tomorrow."

"You said it would take an hour," I whined. "They kept me like a prisoner."

"Next time you just say 'I gotta go.'"

"I did say that."

"Say it louder this time. Meet me at eight, okay?"

We drove for a while, and I wondered how this kid could afford cab rides. Probably the driver was a friend of his, or he was also getting a cut of the deal, or perhaps he was paid by the timeshare company, for reasons beyond me. The extent of the operation spread like a net, and it seemed to cover the whole town. I didn't want to hear about timeshares anymore, but I agreed to one more session. A job's a job. I gave my word. I needed the money. I was going to have to start taking responsibility for my life.

I met Rudy the next morning, took his fifty pesos. An hour after the deluxe breakfast buffet, I stood at a desk a lot like yesterday's. "I'm sorry to waste your time, but I've got to go."

Today's version of Dick looked up from the papers and pictures. "You can't do that," he said.

"Watch me," I replied, and opened the office door, strode into the lobby and finally began to jog because I felt certain a guard would tackle me and drag me back.

"What about your gift?" Dick Two called, hot on my tail. Then I burst through grand double doors, sprinted between twin fountains, and kept on, all the way to a bus stop half a block away, where I waited with the hotel help to be brought back into town.

I avoided Rudy's kiosk the rest of the day, intending to keep the fifty pesos for my trouble, but finally the weight proved too heavy. "What happened to you?" he asked. I pulled out the fifty and set it on his counter, over a photograph of a sailing yacht. He looked at the bill but didn't pick it up.

"I couldn't do it," I said. "Those people…" I searched for words. "They're crazy."

"Man, I thought you were tough."

"I thought I was, too," I said, and walked away.

That night I uncapped my tiny commemorative bottle of tequila, sitting on a boardwalk bench facing the three discos. I wasn't willing to pay an entrance fee but hoped to catch a bit of the festive atmosphere. Perhaps I'd see a drunk tossed by a bouncer, or a juicy fight between lovers. I got down a mouthful of the tequila, and a couple of Mexican girls walked by. "Hola," I called, waving my free hand, the other clasped around the bottle on my knee. They looked me over, said good evening and continued on their way. The taller of the two glanced back, met my eye and turned quickly to her friend. I downed another drink, and they returned fifteen minutes later. "Hello again," I said in Spanish. "Are you from Vallarta or visiting?" To my surprise, they stopped to answer my question. The short one, Linda, lived in town, and her friend was staying with her. Linda wore a dress. Her hair came down to her shoulders and her face was pretty but a bit witchy, by which I mean her nose and chin were pointy and her eyes too close together. The taller girl's name was Gaby. She had mussed hair that hung past her ears, very dense and black, a slightly bumped nose, a large mouth with thick lips. She wore sandals, cut-off jeans and a light, flowery shirt that seemed to consist of more than one layer of fabric. I offered tequila. Glued to the cap was a miniature sombrero, around the brim of which was stitched "M-E-X-I-C-O," a different color for each letter. The girls politely declined. I killed the bottle with two wincing gulps and tossed the empty into a trash can—sombrero and all. "Would you care to accompany me down the boardwalk?" I asked. They looked at each other and spoke too rapidly for me to understand.

"Goodbye," Linda said, "it was nice meeting you." And she left Gaby in my care. We walked the length of the boardwalk several times, passing a number of couples over and over who were doing the same thing we were, checking us out as we checked them out. This walk seemed the protocol for men and women who hadn't yet kissed but might like to. Gaby, once she warmed up, talked plenty. I added a few comments here and there, when I was able to follow, which was about a third of the time. Abruptly she yawned. "Bed time," she said, and kissed me on the cheek.

"Meet me here tomorrow night?" I called as she walked away.

"Maybe," she said, flashing a very pretty smile over her shoulder. I watched her go, those thin legs moving her quickly forward, sandals slapping.

The next morning I again passed the painter of names on grains of rice, which reminded me of my interrupted mission to the USA School. "Yes, sir!" he said as I approached, apparently not recognizing me.

"Hello," I said in Spanish. "Could you remind me where the USA School is?"

He frowned, recalling me all too well now. "Calle Guatemala y Jamaica," he said, and waved to a couple passing behind me. "Your name painted on a grain of rice?" he implored them.

I thanked him and took off. I was dressed in sandals, swim trunks, a yellow *guayabera* shirt and a straw hat. Good enough for the USA School, I decided, and walked out of the tourist area and into a neighborhood of poured concrete residences mixed with stores that provided goods and services you couldn't get downtown, like dentistry and bricks. Twenty minutes later, I turned right on Guatemala Street. The USA School was located on a corner, in a two-level building painted white and fronted by a stencil-painted sign. Across the street, a mangy dog nipping at a horse's legs took a hoof to the head. It yelped and stumbled around the street like a drunk, half dead or on the road to wisdom.

A young woman at a desk in the hallway had me sit in a plastic chair. I could hear two classes going simultaneously. Through an open door, I saw a man gesturing expansively. He wore the USA School tee with sleeves rolled up over his shoulders. He moved out of my line of vision, and loud music started up so suddenly I nearly jumped from my seat. It was an anthem backed by synthesized violins and a drum track that sounded like schoolyard sprinklers. Most of the lyrics were too garbled to understand, except when all the students sang along with the chorus: "I'm in love with you, bay-beee!" When the song ended, students of many ages poured out of the room, glancing furtively at me as they passed. Then the secretary introduced me to José Luis Santana himself, owner, proprietor, and teacher. He wore tight jeans and polished cowboy boots. He smiled widely, shook my hand, and spoke quickly in Spanish. I would later learn that José Luis, though he taught it at the basic level, didn't speak much English.

"The pay is two thousand pesos per month, in advance. Class meets five days a week. I teach level one. You'll teach levels two and three. We're very busy right now. You want a job? Come tomorrow morning. Okay?" He slapped me on the back before I could answer. "Think about it." And he was off to teach the next class.

I spent the rest of the day walking up and down the beach, occasionally kicking off my sandals, shedding the shirt, and diving into the water to cool off. At dusk, I bought three cans of beer, two for my shoulder bag and one for my hand. I sat at my usual bench on the boardwalk. To my surprise, Gaby actually showed up. "You're here," I said.

"So are you," she replied.

I offered her a beer. She shook her head and asked for a sip of mine. This time we walked along the beach instead of the boardwalk, which I took as an encouraging development.

I badly wanted to kiss her, but she kept talking and talking. I'd lost the thread long ago and was thinking my own American thoughts when she shook my shoulder until I returned to the moment. "Yes?"

"What was I saying?" she asked.

I had to admit that I didn't know. She brought me back into things, a movie, about some people who dove deep into the ocean and found some kind of water beings. I couldn't believe it. I'd seen that movie too! She transitioned into another movie; I wasn't sure if I'd seen this one because I simply couldn't understand her words. Luckily she didn't quiz me again. Once away from the lights of town, she pulled me to the sand, but instead of embracing me she produced a thin joint from her Oriental hippy purse. She lit up and passed it to me. I hesitated, not a smoker these days, but finally accepted so as not to seem square.

After the second hit, I sat clasping my knees in fear. Every last Spanish word had escaped my mind, and even the thought of trying to remember one froze me stiff. Gaby, fortunately, didn't notice. She was blathering, waving the burning joint like a sorcerer etching lines of fire onto the night sky, speaking of something grand and interesting and completely beyond my ability to understand. I didn't like her confidence. It scared me. What did she see in me, I began to wonder, a guy who spoke like a child? What was she after? Money? A green card? How long would it take before she started demanding dollars for her dope habit? And then what? Marriage, of course. Soon I'd have to take her back to the States, where she'd secretly invite twenty-five cousins to live with us, one of them a lover in disguise! I'd be a fool, another proud man brought down by the wiles of a woman. I stood abruptly. "I have to go," I managed in Spanish.

She looked up at me, a line of smoke rising from her pinched fingers. "Adios," she said. I turned and fled across the sand, followed by her laughter rising over the gentle growl of the ocean.

The next morning, the secretary, Blanca, handed me a stack of worksheets and a video tape, and sent me into the classroom. I'd never taught before, not on my own. A real teacher had been in attendance when I'd volunteered with Brett back in San Francisco. But I knew that teachers started by introducing themselves, and then the younger ones asked the students to introduce themselves in turn, a way to make them feel that they too were important to the process. "What's your name and what do you do?" I asked them in Spanish and then in English. "Hello," I replied to each in turn, "nice to meet you." We had a kid who worked at a travel agency, an old ranchero who told me in Spanish that he was the night watchman at the USA School and liked to hunt *javalina*, many sullen high school kids obviously there against their wills, a cab driver, and the very same painter of names on grains of rice who'd directed me here.

"I'm not sure how this usually works," I admitted, and the travel agent, who spoke excellent English, told me that I played the tape and then the students filled out the worksheets and finally we'd all go over the material together. I did as told, and before I knew it one class was filing out and another coming in.

Over the siesta break a few hours later, José Luis treated the teachers and staff—me, an American couple from rural Washington, a well-dressed Mexican man on hiatus from timeshare, and Blanca—to a mariachi lunch. After settling the bill, he handed me two thousand pesos cash, and a copy of a CD featuring himself on vocals. It was the music I'd heard in his class. Later I'd learn that purchase of the CD was required for graduation. I walked out of the restaurant, dizzy from three margaritas, a bona-fide teacher of the English language.

By the end of that day's classes, I felt like an old pro. It wasn't so different from waiting tables. I'd stand in front of everyone until I had their attention, but instead of asking what each person wanted to eat and drink, I'd ask a wider variety of questions, moving slowly through the room. I'd make the rounds about three times and class was over. See you tomorrow.

That night, I found Gaby on the boardwalk and apologized for my hasty departure. "I don't smoke much," I admitted.

She shrugged, smiling.

Excited as a teenager, I held her hand as we strolled along the beach, and continued to hold it while walking her home. In the middle of town, a stray dog came scrounging up and she caught it in the side with a deft kick. Those calloused feet had never known a pedicure, I thought with admiration, but they got the job done. We came to a concrete box of an apartment where she was staying with Linda and Linda's boyfriend Marco. The place, with its door wide open, looked dodgy, full of kids lying around on a couch or the floor, a drug den of some sort. Marco, a dude about twenty-five years old, wearing nothing but boxer shorts and an indolent, superior attitude like some low-rent Hugh Hefner, came to the door to shake my hand, radiating malice. I played the clueless gringo rather than take him up on his macho game. "*Mucho gusto*," I said, pumping his hand, scheming to get Gaby out of this place.

I'd been wasting money in a hotel, so I set out to find an apartment. After two days searching, I rented a room a twenty-minute walk inland from the town center. I settled into my new digs for a week, and then took Gaby out to dinner at one of the big taco carts. This one featured several grilled meats—including such exotic fare as brains, "face," and tripe—and two dozen sauces. Gaby began to sweat, downing tacos drenched in a habanero sauce, bright orange like magma. "Whew!" she said, fanning herself, tongue lolling like a dog's. Her hair was plastered to her forehead in little spikes, and I could barely keep from picking her up and kissing her wet face. She saw what I was thinking and we smiled goofily at each other. At the end of the evening, I kissed her beside the door of the drug den. I'd feared she'd play coy when this moment came, but she returned the kiss hungrily, tasting of hot sauce. One hand traveled up my neck and cupped the back of my head, and I ran my own fingers down the bumps of her spine. Her mouth was large and wet, and her tongue was not bashful.

After several minutes, we broke the embrace. *"Buenas noches,"* I said, glad to leave it at this, glad for the old-fashioned chastity of the courtship, the calm patience rising into something big and frightening, like a temple built stone by stone up over the jungle. Usually by this stage with American women I'd known, sex would have been discussed at length if not already enacted, all very businesslike, grown-up and rushed. I glided home as if carried, tasting Gaby in my mouth and smelling her on my hands. A group of young toughs taunted me from a corner near my place, but I only smiled and floated by. I climbed the stairs up the side of the four-story block of a building and entered my new home.

My place took up the entire third story, an open room that would have been called a loft in the U.S. I wasn't ready for bed, so I circled the apartment, reliving the night, wondering what Gaby would think of the space—so much roomier than Marco's. It was the coolest place I'd ever lived, made even cooler by the fact that the owner and locals didn't recognize the coolness. Two pillars held up the ceiling, and the cold-water bathroom was notched out of a corner by an L-shaped wall with a curtain for a door. The kitchen stood behind a tile bar, set up with a propane double-burner stove, a miniature refrigerator and a sink. The apartment was furnished with a couch and a love seat, a table and chairs, and a hard, narrow bed. I sat on the couch, then the love seat, and finally went out onto the balcony to watch the group of family and friends that always gathered in front of the house across the way, lounging on folding chairs, shooting the breeze while kids played in the street. But it was too late for kids tonight. Only a couple of guys, the white-haired matriarch's sons I supposed, sat smoking at a table stocked with fried cornmeal munchies and sodas they sold to neighbors. I turned off the lights and lay awake, thinking of Gaby and watching one of the geckos that lived on my ceiling stalk a moth in the moonlight.

I woke early to a million roosters, having just fallen asleep ten minutes before, or so it seemed. I was so sleepy I didn't even dread the cold water that fell from the bare shower pipe and gripped my head like a large, strong hand. I danced about, soaping and rinsing as I dodged into and out of the water until more or less clean. I dried and dressed in my usual costume of khaki pants rolled up over the ankles, tire-tread huaraches, lime-green guayabera shirt, and a short-brimmed straw hat. I slung my Huichol-woven *moral* bag over my shoulder, gulped the rest of my instant coffee, and set out, down the stairs and inland, uphill. I climbed a long, crumbling and crooked stairway up the cliff to the highway that bypassed town, where I flagged the first northbound bus. We approached the tunnel cut through the hillside, and I held my breath. It took about a minute to get through the tunnel, which was unventilated and full of fumes. On the other side, I called "*baja*," and the driver glanced into the mirror to see if I was old or feeble. He met my gaze and slowed enough for me to hop out. At a break in the traffic, I sprinted across the road and walked back down from the hillside, through a graveyard full of fading, pastel monuments. Two blocks later, I entered the school. Blanca had my photocopies ready for the day's first class. "Good morning, Teacher," the students sang.

"Good morning," I said. "Are you ready to have some fun?"

◆

Just before sundown on Friday, after weeks of kissing and petting, I met Gaby at Marco's lair. She'd agreed to dinner at my place. For the occasion, I'd broken the bank for jumbo shrimp, chayote, peppers, mangos, jicama, limes, Cazadores tequila, Curacao, and Squirt soda. We walked hand in hand along the dirt path beside a muddy stream that drizzled down the hills and into town. Soon we came to the edge of El Caloso, my neighborhood, guarded as always by the teenagers at the corner, who almost never missed a chance to harass me. Sure enough, one of them meowed like a cat as we passed. His buddies giggled.

"Here we are," I said, letting her in. The south wall was floor to ceiling sliding glass doors, which I always left open to the balcony facing the street. Orange sheets decorated with red swirls had been hung as curtains, and tonight they flew in the breeze like banners. I took Gaby by the elbow and led her to the small kitchen window. Silently, I pointed out the big old iguana on his usual limb of the mango tree just outside, head raised toward the setting sun, as if he were warming his throat.

"How ugly!" Gaby said, and the sensitive beast scurried away into the leaves.

I mixed my version of a margarita: tequila, Curacao, fresh lime juice and a splash of Squirt, pronounced locally, "*esquirté.*" I salted the rims and served them up. "Health," I said, and touched my glass to Gaby's. "Sit down, relax," I said, pulling out a bar stool. She watched as I chopped chayote and sautéed it in olive oil. While it sizzled, I sliced a cucumber and cubed a jicama. I added peppers to the chayote and began to heat oil in a second pan. I dropped in a pad of butter and arranged the shrimp in concentric circles from the outside in. By the time I got to the middle it was time to flip the outside layer. Salt, pepper, lime juice, and the local

Salsa Huichol. The Valentina salsa, a bit more citrusy, less smoky, was better suited to the cold cucumbers and jicama, which I served up with plenty of lime and salt. I set the plates on the table, kissed the salt off Gaby's lips, and we settled down to eat. The sun set, and the wind died, bringing the waving curtains to rest. For dessert, we split a mango. Gaby ate hers like she ate everything: dipped in salt and sprinkled with Huichol and lime.

Experience had taught me that things rarely worked out the way I'd planned them. Senior prom. New Year's Eve. A visit from an old friend. Funerals. I never seemed to feel the way I was supposed to feel, and when I did feel the right way, the other people involved didn't act accordingly. So I wasn't expecting to have sex with Gaby, even though every aspect of the night was meant to lead to that. I was prepared for more frustration; I even looked forward to not getting what I wanted, in a puritanical, masochistic way. My job, as the male of the species, was to try my best. Hers was to put me off as long as possible. At some point it would all come to a head, probably when I didn't expect it. Tonight was just part of that process.

We wiped the mango from our faces, and I led Gaby to the couch. We necked like school kids, and then lay down. I was on top of her, nestled between her legs, propped on my elbows so as not to crush her. Her eyes were closed and her mouth slightly parted. My shorts chafed, but I couldn't stop moving against her, or rather, didn't want to stop. I kissed her salty neck and slowly raised her tank top, above her belly and over her bra. She lifted her arms, either like Super Girl taking flight or the villainess surrendering to the sheriff. She leaned forward so I could unclasp the basic white bra. I'd cupped and caressed and even tweaked the nipples of her breasts before, but I hadn't seen them bare. They were palm-sized, creamy pale, with nipples the size of quarters. I kissed one, and then—for symmetry, or perhaps even fairness—the other.

A few minutes later, I sat up and pulled the powder-blue guayabera over my head, smelled a tang from my own underarms. The head of my dick was poking just over the waist of my shorts, like a creature that wanted to see what was going on. Gaby and I slithered against one another shirtless until I couldn't take it any longer, and I unbuttoned her cut-off jean shorts. Down they came, along those long, brown legs. I stood and dropped my shorts. Gaby rolled to her side and stared. She reached out and touched the tip with her index finger. She giggled when it came away with a sticky strand. I hunkered down between her legs and licked her belly button, an inny, very tight and too deep to plumb. Down I traveled. I kissed her through the material of her panties, pushing my tongue into the crevice as my hands slid under her butt. My fingers hooked the waistband and I brought the panties down. I slipped them past her ankles, and she dropped her legs to either side of me and covered herself with both hands.

"I've never done this," she said, face turned to the couch back.

"You're a virgin?" I asked, stunned.

"Almost," she said.

I didn't know what that meant, but I liked it. I stood and helped her up, happy to be naked and hard in the cool evening air. I laid her on the bed and lowered my face between her legs. She moaned, lifted her hips and thrust against me. Later, I slithered up her body. She laughed and wiped my face and tried to escape my wet kisses. I entered her this way, and her laughter ended in a long, open-mouthed breath.

Afterward, we wrapped a curtain around our entwined bodies and stood on the balcony to watch four children play a game below. Three of the kids marched up and down the street in military fashion while the biggest, a girl, paced alongside shouting orders and occasionally smacking the small boy at the end of the line over the head with a rolled newspaper. Gaby unwinded herself from me and crossed the room. She turned on the faucet and began to wash the dishes. I stood behind, cupping her breasts, kissing her neck. She jumped aside and threw a handful of cold water between my legs, and I carried her shrieking and giggling onto the dinner table.

She stayed the weekend. We didn't dress until Sunday night, and then I walked her back to Marco's place. He dealt cocaine, I knew by now. I'd decided his hostility toward me had something to do with Gaby, and I suspected he'd hoped to seduce her on the sly. In any event, I didn't like him, and didn't like Gaby staying with him, but what could I do? Invite her to live with me? I'd known her a month. She was nineteen; I was twenty-nine. We communicated at about the depth that the famous signing chimp could speak to her handlers. We didn't know each other. Or did we? I wasn't even sure what it meant to know someone anymore.

The following Saturday, Gaby informed me that she'd be returning to Guadalajara, where she lived with her mother, an aunt, and various cousins. We'd just finished banana pancakes, and I'd been wondering how hard it would be to clean honey from pubic hair without hot water. "I have no money," she said. "Marco doesn't want me to stay anymore. Also, I miss my mother."

I reached across the table and took her hands. "If you ever want to come back to Vallarta," I said, "you can stay here."

"Honestly?"

"Yes," I said, thinking more along the lines of periodic vacations than until-death commitment. But how to explain that without sounding like a jerk, in a language I hardly spoke? "I don't have much," I said, and this was the truth. My wages barely covered rent and food from the grocery store. A night out at the taco stand was an unsustainable luxury. Forget even a single beer at a tourist bar. "But I'll have food in the fridge, and a place to sleep."

She nodded her head, thinking it over. Her breasts wobbled in the flimsy tank top she wore to bed.

"No bringing anyone else to stay here," I said, now a little alarmed at the invitation I'd just extended. She nodded her head like it meant yes, she'd be back, though I couldn't be sure because she didn't seem sure. It was an idea.

She left on Monday while I was teaching. I didn't know what to do with myself that night, and so I circled my apartment, imagining conversations with her, and then with my mother, and my father, and even a long talk with Rachel, an apology for how I'd handled things. Everyone understood, and forgave or were forgiven.

That weekend, I watched a guy juggling clubs on the boardwalk, surrounded by a large audience. My father had actually taught me the basic three-object juggle when I was small, and so I figured to try my hand with clubs. On the way home, I scrounged three plastic one-liter Pepsi bottles, narrow bottles of thick plastic, unlike the fat flimsy ones in the States. At the apartment, I cut off the mouths of the bottles and duct taped to the ends pieces of cardboard tubing from a paper towel roll. The handles were a little floppy, but overall the bottles functioned. An hour later, I could manage a few rotations, and I began to walk the familiar path around my apartment, hugging the wall except where the bed was pushed against it, practicing this mindless, repetitive skill. Soon it was night, and I'd gotten to twenty-two catches. I dropped down for fifty pushups. I had too much energy, felt too good, but I didn't have anything to do with all that power. "How are you today?" I asked a gecko on the wall. "And you guys?" I asked the line of big, black ants that traveled to and from my kitchen sink once a day. "Everything looks alright," I said, and picked up the Pepsi clubs for another go.

◆

For a week I expected Gaby to appear any moment. For another week I hoped. After three weeks I figured she wasn't coming back. Meanwhile, I'd all-but memorized the worksheets and videos at the USA School. The old night watchman, the hunter of javalina, sat in every class I taught but never uttered a single word of English. The high school students didn't do much better. I'd become friends with a couple of teachers from the school, nature people from rural Washington. Americans, one white and the other of Asian heritage, they dressed in beads and fringe, brushed their teeth with licorice twigs, and smoked a lot of pot. They were nice folk, but we weren't of the same tribe. Now and then I'd meet promising tourists at the beach, but I could never keep up with the money they'd casually spend, and so I quit talking to tourists.

Then one Saturday night, too lonely and bored for the austerity program, I dug a crisp $20 from my stash and set out, torpedoes be damned. I proved a hit at the various bars I visited, supplied with months of charm saved up and ready to burn. In no time I was cheerfully drunk, lugubrious and making friends at will. The tourists found me dashing, an Indiana Jones character in my exotic garb and glib Spanish. I did nothing to dispel the illusion. After squeezing every last centavo from the twenty, I came wobbling home after midnight. The boys on the corner slept against one another like monkeys.

I hummed "I Will Survive," a song lip-synched on stage earlier that night by a man in drag. It had been one of those nights where everything happens: drag queens on parade, gregarious hookers, a bar brawl. I'd even spent the last half hour kissing a brunette cutie from Baltimore, whose name I'd never registered.

"I should have changed that stupid lock, I should have made you give your keys," I whisper-sang, trying to get my own key into the lock. "If I'd have known for just one second you'd be back to bother me! Oh no not I!" I finished, stumbling across the threshold, nearly running into Gaby, who stood grinning before me. She looked great, grown-up and sexy in makeup, a short skirt, high sandals and a tight shirt of some shiny material.

I shook my head as if to clear the hallucination, but it was no dream. That was Gaby. "Miguel let me in," she said. Miguel was the landlord. I scooped her up and swung her around until I grew dizzy and almost lost my grip. "Happy Valentine's Day," she said.

"Valentine's?" I asked. I hadn't been paying attention to holidays.

I looked around and saw that not only was Gaby back, but she'd brought a duffle bag that about covered the couch. She'd come to stay. Suddenly weary from the night's adventures, I fell onto the bed, thinking nothing, but feeling very good, very good and very lucky the brunette hadn't come home with me.

Chapter Nine

Mesilla

I left work angry. Blanca had copied Level One worksheets for the Level Three class. I don't even teach Level One, I'd shouted in the hallway. She'd retorted, and I'd responded sarcastically. Later in class I could tell, by the subtly reproachful glances and reluctant participation, that the students took Blanca's side. Nobody wanted to answer my questions, so I began to call on the weakest students in an irritated, impatient voice that didn't improve morale. "Doesn't anyone aside from Benjamin have any idea what's going on?" I'd finally asked. Even class-star Benjamin cringed.

The real reason for the anger, I figured on the way home, holding my breath in the toxic tunnel, was money. "*¡Baja!*" I shouted on the other side, and hopped out as the bus slowed. Cheap as we lived, without luxuries or diversions, the numbers just weren't adding up. Every month I had to extract another bill from my stash, no matter how frugal I tried to be. What would happen when I ran out of greenbacks? I couldn't stand the thought of moving to one of Vallarta's tomb-like apartments. The roomy loft, with its geckos, ants and resident iguana, was the only pleasure left me down here. If I wasn't allowed to go out and spend money, I at least needed the space to circle around. I needed windows letting in the breeze. I needed to keep track of Doña Antonia's family down below, my version of TV.

I heard Gaby's music a block before I got home. Her prized

possession, trucked here from Guadalajara, was a small boom box, which she played constantly, on maximum volume. She liked a style of music called *romantico*, sappy crooners backed by synthesized string instruments, turned up so loudly the cheap speakers warbled and squealed. I walked in on her sweeping great clouds of dust into the air, singing along with lyrics I could never understand no matter how hard I listened.

My urge was to snap off the music and say something nasty. Instead, I left before she'd noticed me. I walked into town and bought a forty-ounce bottle of beer at a convenience store near the beach. At least the ocean is free, I thought, and sat in the sand, beginning to calm down. Large waves boomed as I twisted the cap. Had the swell covered the reassuring sound of released pressure? I brought the bottle to my nose and sniffed. No hops, no barley. No smell at all. Hands trembling with impending rage, I braved a sip, and sure enough, I tasted nothing but water.

I burst into the store and shoved the bottle at the girl behind the counter, a fat teenager with racoonish black makeup around her eyes. "This is full of water," I said.

Her face was blank, as if she couldn't understand my gringo tongue. I'd encountered this tactic before, so I repeated myself word by word, enunciating as to a child or an imbecile.

"There is no beer in this bottle. It is filled with water."

She pursed her lips while shrugging and tilting her raccoon face to one side, absolving herself utterly.

"Someone in this store," I said, my voice rising, "drank this beer, replaced it with water, and you sold it to me,. just two minutes ago! I want a fresh bottle, or my money back."

Lips still pursed, she shook her head slightly, the minimum movement required to make her point. I imagined smashing the bottle over her head and stabbing her throat with the shards. Instead, I stormed out and upended the bottle just outside the open door. The water gurgled onto the sidewalk in a pitifully slow trickle. When it was finally empty, I returned and demanded my deposit. She put a peso coin on the counter. I snatched it up and stomped away, composing a vicious letter in my mind, which I'd publish in *Vallarta Today*, warning gringo tourists away from this den of inequity. Especially watch out for the girl with black eye makeup, I'd write. Soon after publication, business would plummet, and later I'd pass the store, now empty and for sale. Eventually, I'd run into the girl, unemployed, homeless, begging for food on the corner. I'd give her a peso—the very same coin she'd given me! Then I'd calmly explain to her about the virtues of good old American-style customer service, how in the long run it paid off. No wonder Mexico's economy was always in the dump! I thought. When would they learn?

"We need to talk," I demanded when I got home.

"Where have you been?" Gaby asked.

"At the beach, but that doesn't matter. Two things. One, you've got to get a job."

"Okay," she said.

"I can't pay for everything around here."

"Okay."

"I'm going to run out of money, and then what?"

"I don't know."

"It doesn't have to be a great job. Just something to help out with food a little."

"I'll start looking tomorrow."

"Yes. Good. The second thing is, I need to get out of here."

I explained over Gaby's frown that my tourist visa, good for six months, was about to expire. My plan was to cross the border and return for a new stamp. She didn't appear to understand, and I wasn't quite sure either. I had no idea what the penalty for an expired tourist visa was. I didn't even know who would check the stamp, expired or otherwise. On the other hand, I'd heard what happened to gringos in Mexican jail, even for minor offenses. They'd lock you up and squeeze your American relatives for bribes, dragging out the process for years. Meanwhile, the gangsters inside would treat you to daily beatings and worse. Would the guards protect you? Not on your life. They hated gringos as much as anyone. Thus, I needed a stamp.

A few days later, I told José Luis about my problem. Without hesitation, he granted me a leave of absence. If he couldn't find someone to replace me, he'd simply offer fewer classes next term. So with a familiar sense of excitement and possibility, I packed the Marrakesh, left Gaby in charge of the apartment, and boarded a bus for Guadalajara. A feeling of peace settled over me in the train to Mexico City. Something about moving, particularly away from responsibilities, always lightened my spirit. Savoring the quiet and solitude, I spent the hours looking out the window, writing in a notebook, reading, or walking the length of the train to check out the other passengers.

Two days later, I ate fried grasshoppers in Oaxaca's *zocalo*. They were crunchy and salty and hardly recognizable as insects. Munching away, I recalled popular John's speech about people who ate insects. At last, I'd joined them, the bug eaters of the world. I wondered what John would think if he saw me now, the quiet kid with a bad haircut, now a world traveler!

Next I came to San Cristobal de las Casas, capital of Chiapas. This territory belonged to the Zapatistas, the rebel group so often in the news back then. They were a peaceful movement, interested more in labor stoppages than acts of terror, in spite of their ominous black hoods. Their spokesman was a blue eyed man who called himself Subcomandante Marcos, *Subcomandante* instead of *Comandante* because he believed a non-indigenous should never be considered the leader of the movement. Rumor had it that he was a political science professor from Mexico City, and the discussion over breakfast at the pension focused on whether he was a meddling yuppie or a hero. I personally couldn't see the problem.

So what if he taught in Mexico City? So what if his eyes were blue? He seemed to be doing a pretty good job, and the other Zapatistas apparently liked him well enough. But I didn't feel like getting into it, so I finished my corn flakes and set off for Guatemala.

Supplied with a change of clothes, toiletries, a notebook, bottle of water, and *The Natural* by Barnard Malamud, I crossed the border. After the usual complications and delays, I arrived by bus in a village called Mesilla, a small collection of huts that lined a muddy road off the highway. It featured no bars or restaurants, certainly no movie theater. I had figured to spend the night in Guatemala, to put on a good show for the visa stamp, but Mesilla had no hotel, and I didn't know how long I'd have to travel to find a bigger city. Hot and damp, exposed in the center of the dirt road that cut through town, I entered the biggest building in the village, a Catholic church painted canary yellow. Inside it was empty, dark and somber. I sat on a pew in the back and leaned forward as if to pray, thinking that this was the type of village where the American tourist had been beaten a few years ago.

Faced with a suffering Jesus behind the pulpit, I recalled the day my mother brought Ole and me to the little chapel in Anza. Five years old, I'd sat there stunned, uncomprehending and despairing that the grownups had figured out yet another way to torture me. First school, I was thinking, now this! After a joyless hour of standing and sitting, listening to an old man drone, and singing songs that brought no one pleasure, two men passed silver donation plates up and down the rows. When the plate went by us, Ole grabbed a handful of coins. Mom laughed and told him to let go. The people around us smiled, but I could feel humiliation rising like fever on my cheeks. Ole looked at Mom, a little boy betrayed, fingers white around the coins. "Come on," she said, losing patience. Ole fought with every muscle he had, until Mom pried open his fists, and the money clanked onto the plate.

"Nooooooooooo!" he howled. "Nooooooooooo!" We got out of there fast. Years later, Mom told me that the priest had recommended that she not come back. Not because of Ole's outburst, of course. He didn't like the way we dressed. The world was changing. The scruffy types with their long hair and loose morals were taking over. He must have seen the church as a last bastion of righteousness, must have felt he was protecting his flock, protecting some idea he had about the way things should be. I considered how my mother must have felt, banned from the house of God, and I hated the small-minded preacher a little. Then it occurred to me that, old then, the man was long dead by now, and I forgave him. He'd been scared, and now he was gone.

My thoughts turned to The Walk, the church Mom had run to after that first shot at religion. For a while, I'd been one of them, a convert. I'd shout the angry taunts at Satan, right along with the grownups. I'd even "worship," with arms aloft, moaning mumbo jumbo while swaying side to side, though never without a sense, slight at first but ever growing, of self consciousness, of not believing even as I told myself I believed, of not quite giving in, a subtle feeling of embarrassment, as if, right at the moment of letting go, curtains would part and the host of Candid Camera would burst forth laughing, revealing the whole thing as an elaborate joke, meant to make a fool of me. The question of my faith came to a head in one of the Walk mega churches. All those who hadn't experienced a "laying on of hands" were encouraged to walk up to the stage, where the pastor clutched the worshipper's head with both hands, forcing him to stagger, to stumble, to drop to his knees and be saved. I stood in line, twelve years old, craving the approval of these people, wanting above all else to belong, but then the line moved forward, and I did not. Several people in the audience turned and smiled, urging me on with waves of their hands. "It's okay," one man said. "Don't be afraid." But I was afraid, afraid to walk forward, to submit to the pastor's hands on my head, to fall down to my knees, to be saved. It seemed a crucial moment, too important to fake, because God would surely see right through to my false heart. So I turned around and slunk to the back of the building, to wait out the rest of the service, hating myself and the church.

After that, services began to seem silly, even ugly. The pastors and elders were bullies, the rest submissive weaklings. I detected in the church a familiar pyramid-shaped structure, in which a few enjoyed the view from the backs of everyone else. I felt like a hypocrite, sitting in the back row, resenting the dullness and wasted time, criticizing the whole show in my head. I stood my ground on a Sunday. As Mom and Ralph prepared for church, I locked myself in the bathroom. When it was time to go, I refused to open the door. Mom was shocked first, and then furious. Ralph threatened to break down the door, but Mom stopped him at the last moment. After shouts and threats from both sides of the door, they left with stunned Ombleo. While they were gone, I packed a bag and left home, eventually ending up at a friend's house, where I stayed for a few days until Mom tracked me down. We talked on the phone, both of us tearful and apologetic by this time. Back home, they never asked me to attend church again, but an invisible wall began to grow from that day on between my mother and me. I wanted freedom, and I got it. But there was a price. No such thing as a free lunch.

God, I thought, closing my eyes and resting my head in my arms on the bench back. I feel stupid talking to you because I don't believe you're up there listening. But I used to pray, and I've got some time to kill, so why not? I hope you understand why I can't buy the idea of you. It's just kind of unlikely, don't you think? Kind of convenient, how you're a lot like us, and you always seem to want us to do things that are good for the people who speak for you, like giving them money, or supporting their wars against people whose land they want to take. Anyway. I mean no disrespect. Just telling the truth, and if you're the kind of god I'd bother to pray to, you respect the truth. So if you're around and listening, please give my brother some wisdom. He's not a bad guy. Just screwed up. He got a raw deal, it seems to me, and I know I didn't help matters any, being a bad influence with my pot smoking and screwing around. Also, heal my mother, or at least convince her to get that operation. She could use some easy years about now. And if you're giving stuff away, I wouldn't mind a little something myself, but I'm not sure what it is right now. A job might be nice, but that sounds lame. Might as well ask for a million dollars. I guess I'd like to do something worthwhile and interesting with my life. Never mind. Don't worry about me. You've got bigger problems. Amen.

I rose and left the chapel.

At the border station in Mexico, a pumpkin-headed guard stamped my passport without even glancing at the other pages. Back in San Cristobal, I decided on a different route to Vallarta, up through the Caribbean city of Vera Cruz and west to Mexico City, making a big loop of my trip. After two days of travel, I stopped at a large campground outside of the ruins of Palenque, a much later Mayan city than Tikal, more ornate, according to my guidebook. The campground was packed with young travelers: Americans, Europeans, South Africans, Australians and New Zealanders, white people on tight budgets. While the look was decidedly scruffy, the atmosphere was like that of a big frat party, with everybody drinking, smoking, shouting, and trying to get laid. They were also, I later learned, consuming great amounts of hallucinogenic mushrooms, one of the principal draws of Palenque.

I was assigned to share a palapa with an Australian guy, drunken and maudlin. He sat rocking with his head in his hands. "My parents think I'm a loser," he said without looking up. As I strung my hammock, he explained how he'd been vagabonding for seven years. When he ran out of money, he'd head to London or some other international city and work in a bar, bedding down in a tiny apartment with a bunch of other wanderers. "After a while," he said, "you get plugged into the traveler network, and it's easy." As soon as he replenished the bank account, he'd set out again, seeking cheap accommodation and the next party. His name was Charlie, and his immediate plan was to make his way north to the Alaska fisheries for a season. They paid well and you couldn't spend money stuck out there. The only problem was that a few people fell into the water and died each season, but Charlie would risk it. He had nothing to lose.

"Ah, shit," he said, and slugged his bottle of beer. "I'm pissing my life away."

"But you're seeing the world," I told him.

"No I'm not. You've seen one pub, you've seen them all. That's what my father told me. And you know what? He's right."

"What about...I don't know, culture? How about these ruins?"

"I don't give a rat's ass about the ruins. I came for the mushies."

"How about Spanish?" I said. "Learning a new language does great things for your mind. It's like doubling the world."

"I don't know a fuckin' word of Spanish."

"I'll teach you. Come on."

"Forget it," he said. "I won't remember anyway. Beside, I'll be in some other country where they don't speak Spanish in a few days. I can't learn every language, so why bother?"

By late night, the party had died out around the edges and concentrated at a big bonfire in the center of the campground, mainly occupied by a large contingency of hard-drinking Kiwis. I lay rocking in my hammock for hours, drifting in and out of sleep. When dawn broke, I got up, washed my face and brushed my teeth. The Kiwis lay around the ashes, dropped in their clothes, some of them still clutching jumbo beer bottles. The scene looked like a cult mass suicide.

I left the campground, following the dirt road that cut through the jungle to the ruins. Fifty feet ahead, the trees rustled and out popped a little brown man in rags. He waved me forward, looking around in an exaggerated expectation of trouble. I couldn't help smiling. His short stature and shyness brought to mind a leprechaun, or perhaps, as they called magical little people down here, a *duende*. I approached without fear. I just couldn't believe this guy would lead me into an ambush. He was too comical for that.

As I drew near, he retreated half into the forest, some kind of woodland spirit. I came to him and he shoved a brown paper lunch bag into my hand. I unrolled the top and looked in. The bag was half full of mushrooms. "Twenty, twenty," the duende said in English.

"Pesos?" I asked, and he nodded vigorously. I wasn't sure what to do with the mushrooms. Certainly I had no urge to eat them anytime soon. On the other hand, I couldn't pass up a large bag of psychedelic mushrooms for two dollars. They'd be worth fifty easy in the States. I dug into my pockets while the duende gestured impatiently, urging me to speed things up. It registered only deeply in my mind that this was a drug deal. I gave him two tens, and he disappeared into the woods. Bag stashed in my day pack, I continued on into the ruins.

The park was quite small compared to Tikal. The surrounding jungle was similarly innocuous, a mere fifty-feet high and not nearly as dense as Guatemala's Peten. The place didn't scare me like Tikal had, didn't intimidate me. I sensed no ghosts. By lunchtime, I'd seen as much as I wanted to see. Back at the camp, packing, I said goodbye to Charlie, who was still half asleep in his hammock. He only faintly remembered meeting me the night before, and his formerly low opinion of himself had been replaced by a sleepy contentment. I told him about the duende, and my plan to bring the mushrooms back to Vallarta, to share them with Gaby and a couple we'd befriended. None of us were dopers, but for some reason mushrooms—the fact that they grew naturally, and that we ate various non-psychedelic versions in salads and on burgers—didn't seem to qualify as a drug.

"You need to dry those things," Charlie said. "Or better yet, pack them in honey. They'll turn if you don't."

I wished Charlie luck and took off, thinking to keep my eye out for honey, though I hadn't seen a grocery store since Mexico City. In the meantime, the mushrooms were rolled in their brown bag, stuffed in a sock, and shoved deep into the Marrakesh. I'd be home in four days. Surely they'd hold out until then.

I traveled without incident, by bus to Vera Cruz, a dreary port city as far as I could see, and then on to gigantic and inscrutable Mexico D.F. I spent the overnight train ride to Guadalajara reading *The Natural*, which I'd picked up in the San Cristobal pension. I'd seen the movie based on the novel, and because of that I'd been expecting heroic schlock. What I found instead was lyricism and black, cynical comedy. It seemed as if the filmmakers had read the book and set out to create the Bizarro World version of the story, the exact opposite of the writer's intentions. Somehow this fact seemed to support the novel's critique of America. After each chapter, I'd walk the length of the train, sizing up the new passengers, noting who had gone. A mustachioed man wearing a yellow cowboy shirt wished me a good evening as I passed. It was the closest thing to a conversation I had all night.

I finished the book long after most passengers had fallen asleep, a period of time—roughly after midnight and before dawn—called the *madrugada*, a word I found beautiful and apt, and which had no precise counterpart in English. I lay my head back and rocked with the train, thinking of old days, back when I'd been a baseball-obsessed boy, throwing a tennis ball against the side of the Anza cabin for hours at a time, practicing my backhand grab. Eventually, I'd joined a series of Little League teams, and settled into second base and shortstop. I dreamed of making the Majors all the way through ninth grade, up until I'd begun to smoke pot and dream darker dreams. I drifted from the bitterness of old regrets into light sleep.

In the morning, we pulled into the terminal in Guadalajara. From here, I'd catch a three-hour bus to Vallarta. I wondered how I'd find the apartment. A total mess? A bunch of druggies having moved in? Gaby gone? Marco finally having his way with Gaby in my bed? I was walking along the platform beside the train, shaking my head to rid it of stupid fears, when someone touched my shoulder. "Yes?" I asked, turning to a man wearing a large cowboy hat. I recognized his mustache and yellow shirt from the train, and I figured I must have left something behind. He pulled a billfold from his back pocket and opened it to a silver badge.

"May I search your bag?" he asked in English.

It hadn't occurred to me, not really, that transporting hallucinogenic drugs from Palenque to Vallarta was a crime. Trafficking them across the border into America was a crime, of course, but keeping them inside Mexico had seemed like carrying a drink from one side of a night club to another. But now I understood that Mexico wasn't a nightclub. It was a country, with laws and police to enforce those laws. A vision of prison rose around me as I slipped the pack from my shoulders, concrete walls pushing up through the ground, and a roof blocking the sun. This is it, I thought, as a storm began to rage in my chest, time to not fuck up. I laid the pack on the platform, trembling inside. "Go ahead," I said, smiling while my heart pounded so hard I thought the cop would see my shirt flutter. I looked down at the pack, deflated beside his snakeskin cowboy boots.

"What are you doing in Mexico?" he asked, slowly unzipping the bag.

"Traveling," I said, "working on my Spanish. Mi Español." I laughed humbly at the paucity of my Spanish.

"Oh?" He poked through clothes, lifting and looking around.

"I finished college last year," I went on. "Studied a little Spanish, but you can't learn it if you don't live it. That's what I believe."

He looked up. We were both squatting, facing one another across the bag, which lay open like a gutted beast. He stared into my eyes, and I saw the pores on his nose as big as lunar craters. I made my vision go soft and unfocused, not staring but not avoiding his gaze either. "I trust you," he said.

Really? I almost replied. I had to keep myself from throwing my arms around his neck. "Thank you," I said casually. "I appreciate that."

"Enjoy your trip." He stood and walked away.

I stayed down a moment longer, careful not to zip the bag too eagerly, letting the fact sink in. I wasn't going to jail. I'd screwed up but wasn't going to pay for it. I considered my recent talk with God. Thank you, I thought, not that I believe in you.

Back in Vallarta, I walked the familiar route through town, along the stream that traversed the bit of wilderness between "Old Town" and El Caloso. "*Güero*," one of the corner kids said. "Where have you been? Smoking weed?" The others laughed.

"No weed for me," I said. "I found God."

I threw open the door. Gaby ran across the room and hugged me. The place was strewn with clothes and junk she'd brought from Guadalajara. "I'm glad to be home," I told her, and this was certainly true. I didn't ask whether she'd found a job because I already knew the answer, and didn't want to get into it so soon.

The following night, I brought the mushrooms to my friend Mark's place in town. I dumped what had become a slimy stew onto a plate in the kitchen. "*¡Wacala!*" cried Gaby, an expression that meant what it sounded like. Individual stems and caps could no longer be identified in the sticky mass of chunky brown mucus. The stuff smelled like bleach.

"Is this safe?" Mark's girlfriend asked.

"No problem," said Mark, a rugged Australian. He helped me split the gunk onto four salad plates. We stood around the kitchen table, gathering nerve. "Bottoms up," Mark said, and used his fingers to slide the slime into his mouth, as one eats a raw oyster on the shell. The rest of us followed his lead. I retched, swallowed, and chased it with several gulps of beer.

"That was the most disgusting thing I've ever eaten," Mark's girlfriend said, and we all agreed.

A half hour later the four of us were strolling, tingling and giggly along the beach, watching waves so soft and playful they must have been made of frosting. The moon, three quarters full and hovering over the water, cast its light like spilled milk on the ocean, and the music from the three discos joined in a happy kind of madness. "Thank you," I muttered, watching a wave's face flash green from glowing diatom plankton. I held Gaby close and breathed in the scent of her hair, damp and salty from ocean mist.

"For what?" Gaby asked.

"What?"

"Why, 'thank you'?"

"Oh," I said, thinking back to a moment before, when the wave hadn't yet broken. Now the foam bubbled and sloshed. "Nothing. I was talking to myself," I said, and began to laugh, helplessly and for no good reason.

Chapter Ten

Three Arch Bay

I was preparing the bottom-floor studio for Dad, about a week before his release. Back in Vallarta, I'd finally run out of money, gave up the apartment, and accompanied Gaby back to her place in Guadalajara. Her mother and aunt welcomed me warmly, but we all knew that Gaby and I would be parting ways. I couldn't stay in Mexico—or wasn't willing to on a USA School wage—and she didn't have the means or legal right to leave.

Not that she hadn't tried to leave Mexico in the past. Showing me around her old stomping ground, she pointed out the office building where she and a friend had signed up for a program that sent young Mexican women to Japan to work as waitresses. Gaby was making final preparations for the trip when a news report exposed the program as a front for a human trafficking ring that sold poor, venturesome girls like Gaby into sexual slavery. No free lunch in Mexico either.

When it was time for me to go, Gaby accompanied me to the bus station. We kissed goodbye without tears or drama, acting as if we'd somehow meet again. It was easier that way.

Gil and Helen picked me up from the Amtrak station in San Juan Capistrano; as always, their spare room was open to me. Helen was especially glad to have me around for Dad's release. For my part, I poked about for jobs, but mostly I waited, soaking in the comfort of Casa

CLOUDBREAK, CALIFORNIA

Three Arch.

I stocked the studio with towels, toiletries, and bedding, and then I set up a stereo system I'd found at a yard sale. Finished, I found myself snooping around, not expecting to find anything, but unable to help myself. I checked the drawers in the bathroom and under the sink, the high shelves in the closet, and then the cabinets over the television. I found nothing of interest, just some rolled-up television cable, dust, and cleaning supplies. Then I regarded a painting on the wall, a familiar piece of what Helen called "primitive art." It used to decorate one of the guest rooms of their house in Corona del Mar, where my brother and I had slept during visits. The scene, both colorful and dark, focused on a blazing bonfire, around which danced several half-naked, wild-eyed savages with faces frozen in grimaces of ecstasy or pain. The one in the forefront, a man dressed in a loincloth and a red headscarf, wielded a knife with a large, curved blade; his uplifted eyes were rolled back in his head. The painting had always scared me at night back then, along with the slow searching headlights of cars that would pass through the room and the mournful tolling of the grandfather clock.

A mysterious urge had me pull it off the wall. On the other side, I discovered a seam in the wall paneling, about two-by-two foot square. One side of the panel gave under the pressure of my hand, clicked, and swung open, revealing the dirt crawlspace behind the room and under the rest of the house. And right there, among pipes, joists, and spider webs, lay an old surfboard, plain white, fin up in the chalky dirt. I wrestled it through the opening and laid it on the floor. It was a long, narrow relic from the seventies, called a gun, if I remembered right. The deck was contoured in a thick layer of wax, stained black by long-ago feet. The board smelled like salt and wax, a scent that brought back old times with my dad, pre-dawn surf journeys to mythic spots whose names every California surfer knew: Old Man's, Swami's, Trestles…Timbuktu, Shangri -La, El Dorado.

During a summer visit when I was nine, Dad and his blonde, long-haired buddy Jeff, the original Spicoli, were hanging out in a trailer where Dad lived at the time. I sat on the sandy futon petting my dad's three legged husky, Duke, and listening. The talk, as always, was of waves: where they were coming from, how big, what shape, where they were heading. Dad and his friends could go on for hours. Sometimes they'd offer sacrifices to the ocean—old boards, trinkets, spare change—asking for surf. On this night, after listening to the weather report on the radio, Dad got it into his head that the swell would hit Rincon, way up in Santa Barbara. Jeff agreed. Suddenly it was bedtime.

Dad woke me an hour before dawn. He threw an extra board and a small wetsuit into the back of his truck, along with his and Jeff's gear, and we hit the freeway, beating even the earliest commuters. I sat in the middle, and Duke occasionally stuck his head through the back window to keep tabs on us. An hour into the trip, we crested a rise and looked down on "the valley," a stunning wash of city lights gathered in a dark bowl of surrounding hills. "Always a nice sight," Dad said, and Jeff rolled a joint. I passed it back and forth between Jeff and my dad, gripping it the way I'd seen them grip it, with one finger first, and then pinching the oily end as the other guy let go, something like a secret handshake.

After a quick stop for donuts, we parked on the cliff overlooking the long point and half a dozen right-breaking waves peeling off toward the shore, very pretty and very orderly. The sky was pale gray and low, and I counted around twenty black figures waiting in the water or taking off or gliding along the glassy waves. Jeff opened a small plastic box full of gray blobs that looked like used chewing gum. He stuffed one in each ear. I asked if I could have a couple. "You have ear trouble, too?" he shouted.

"Yes," I said, though this wasn't true, as far as I knew. I just wanted to do what he did.

We pulled on our wetsuits, waxed up, and walked down the pathway. My arm was too short to hold the board tucked into my armpit like Dad and Jeff, so I carried it on my head. At the rock-covered shore, we fastened the leashes to our ankles and entered the water. The rocks were slippery and hurt my feet, but soon I shoved off and paddled after Dad. The waves, shoulder-high from the shore, had somehow turned into monsters. Dad lined one up, took off, and rode a few yards before cutting back over the wave and paddling back to where I waited. I kept trying to catch a wave, but they always passed under me. The problem was that I was scared of actually catching the wave, so I'd paddle too far out, and then try to paddle back in to catch it, always a little late. Dad said something, but I couldn't hear because of the ear plugs.

"What? What?" I shouted, thrashing my dead arms to get into place. Dad paddled up next to me. "What'd you say?" I repeated.

"Shhh," he said. "Everyone already knows you don't surf. Let's not attract any more attention than necessary."

I stayed in the water until my fingers were pruned, until finally I caught a nice, smooth wave. Sliding along the easy grade, I hopped to my feet, wavered like a drunkard, kicked the board out in front of me, and back flopped into the water.

"I saw you stand up for a second," Jeff said when we'd gotten back in the truck. Shrugging, I passed the joint to Dad. "It's a start," Jeff added, but I didn't want to start learning to surf. I wanted to surf.

Back in Casa Three Arch, I stared up at the ceiling, which, through some odd whim of Gil's, was mirrored. I saw myself, cropped hair, surf trunks, flannel shirt, and Doc Martin boots, kneeling beside a surfboard and looking up as if imploring the heavens. I could hear the tennis match Gil was watching from his bed one floor up, and I pictured him, hairy and naked except for white briefs, propped against several pillows with a stockpot full of popcorn on his lap. "Thirty love," said the British announcer. Helen was off somewhere playing bridge. I was practically alone, and I liked it, the privacy of Casa Three Arch. There was something sexy, though not strictly sexual, about the moment, a strange, sly thrill I couldn't quite identify. I considered the board, stroking the waxy deck. Clearly, it had been my father's. Probably Helen hadn't had the heart to throw it out when they moved from their last home, but hadn't wanted to see it either. So into the crawlspace it went, out of the way but not gone, like Dad himself.

I carried the board out onto the deck. The beach below was empty, owing to the flat gray sky and chilly November air. For several minutes, I watched the smallish waves occasionally break to the right or left of the rock that stood in the center of the little cove on the south end of Three Arch Bay. I stuck the board under my arm, ran like a burglar up the side of the house to the road, and then a couple of blocks to the beach access stairway.

I sat in sand warmer than the air and pulled off my boots and shirt. At the edge of the water, I squatted and tried to gauge the size, frequency, and angle of the waves, mentally placing myself in the magic spot of each wave as it rose and curled over. They topped out at about three or four feet. Sometimes they broke to the right, sometimes to the left, and other times they "closed out," which meant the whole thing collapsed at once. I realized I was stalling, afraid of cold, failure…drowning. I cleared my throat, fastened the leash, and entered the water. My feet stung, then ached, and finally went numb. The water crept up my legs, and I hopped like a child when it washed over my groin. I waited for the calm between waves, then launched forward on the board, nearly sliding off the deck but righting myself and paddling toward a low wall of foam. I pulled too hard with my right arm and turned sideways as I collided with the wave. The board and I rolled, and I popped to my feet in waist-deep water, sputtering and panting and hopping about from the shocking cold. The board pointed toward the shore like a dog that wanted to go home. I yanked it back, aimed it at the horizon, hopped on and paddled out before the next wave came.

My shoulders already burned with fatigue. I laid my head on my hands and closed my eyes as the ocean undulated softly under me. The next move was to sit up, so I popped right onto my butt like a cowboy on his horse. I sat tall, feeling pretty good about things, but then I leaned a little to one side, then leaned the other way to compensate, and leaned once more before plopping into the water and swimming immediately, as if I'd meant to do just that because I could feel them, the eyes upon me. All along the cliff and up the hillside, dozens, hundreds of watchers behind those opaque windows were all wondering what this lone guy was doing out on such a gray day. Look at him, they said. No wetsuit. Ancient board. He's no surfer!

I climbed back onto the board and took to paddling again. I had this part down fairly well, but my shoulders and chest muscles were about done, and my neck hurt from holding my head up. It was time for another shot at the cowboy position, so I slowly walked my hands up the deck between my legs. I scooted to the center of the board as I rose, found the balance point, and straightened my back. Gentle waves moved under me, and I managed to ride them out with a little hip swivel. Feeling it now, the rhythm of the ocean, I folded my arms across my chest and relaxed. I was in pretty good shape, except that the board had turned around, and I faced the shore, not the horizon. I needed to drop down and start over, but it seemed like too much work. Instead I twisted my neck to look over my shoulder for incoming waves. I felt the cliff-side watchers begin to lose interest, to fade back into their houses and their lives.

The key, I decided, was to relax, so I focused on my stiff shoulders, felt them slowly go loose, then my back, my pelvis. I didn't have to worry about my legs, because I couldn't feel them. Side to side, I gently rocked with the waves, side to side; a sway to the left, a sway to the right, a bit farther to the left, and then even farther to the right. Up top, I was playing it cool, but below my legs were crazy dancing to keep me upright. Finally, I dropped to my belly and began to paddle hard toward the deep water, as if I'd seen it, the big one.

But there was no big one. Not even a small one. I was way too far out, and going farther. The waves broke seventy feet back at the shore, and I was a tiny vessel on the open sea, now mired in a thick bed of kelp. Slimy leaves touched my hands, and the stalks wrapped around my wrists. The water around the plants was black, except for the glistening, rust-colored leaves that emerged and submerged in ripples. I pictured sharks nosing through the forest below, and I jerked my hands from the water and lifted my feet. Now I was stuck, in deep water, a tasty, helpless morsel in the middle of the food chain. I plunged my arms back into the water and tried to turn the board around. The going was too slow with the fin caught in the kelp, so I slid off the board and swam through the scratchy muck. Fear and disgust lent me strength as the slick kelp slithered around my legs and torso. I power stroked back toward shore and broke free. Then I jerked the board out of the kelp by the leash and climbed on.

My arms were stone, the water molasses, and my sore chin kept knocking against the deck. But I got there, into the breaking zone, where I turned the board and sat tall in the saddle, teeth chattering, arms trembling, and chest rubbed raw. The wave approached slowly, calmly, a great lump, rising. I lifted the board's nose while sinking the tail, intending to swing the whole rig around toward the shore. The idea was sound, but I hadn't put enough force into the turn, and so I stalled with my side to the wave as it caught me up and lifted me high. I whimpered at the apex of a churning waterfall, peering down a long drop to the sucking bottom. Then the wave moved on and broke without me.

Before I could thank my stars, another wave moved silently through the kelp. I thrashed the water to get into position. Arms flaming and spent, I forced them to stab the water and drag it back, one and then the other. The wave lifted me from behind, legs above my head as if I'd been caught in a snare. At the crest, I clutched the rails and slid down the gleaming, foam-mottled face, all the way down to the bottom, where the nose sank deep into the base of the wave and my face followed. Still clinging to the board, I bounced, flipped, legs over ass. For a moment, I left the water, and then flopped hard on my back with the board held like a shield against the wave that crashed down and knocked the waxy deck against my nose. I went under and commenced to tumble like clothes in the dryer. Thrashing and frantic, I flailed my arms to catch something, but there was nothing but foam. The leash yanked my ankle, and I didn't know which way was up until I rolled onto sand and lifted my head, panting and sputtering on all fours in six inches of water. I coughed and wiped my face, kneeling before the ocean like a penitent. I struggled to my feet, staggered toward the beach where the board lay fin-down in the damp sand. I shoved it under my arm. Every muscle hot and tight, cold water streaming down my chest and sides, I walked up the beach, aware of each cell in my body, from the arches of my feet to my puckered scalp. Just another surfer, I thought, glancing up at a thousand implacable windows, in from a session.

Chapter Eleven

The Cove

I was watching a sitcom in the den when the garage door began to growl, announcing the arrival of my father, home from Soledad State Penitentiary. The show was stupid, about a bunch of stoned kids who behaved like nobody I'd ever met. I clicked off the television, partly to honor the occasion and partly because I didn't want to be caught watching it. I stood by the door as Gil walked in, resplendent in a royal blue Hawaiian shirt and jet-black mustache and hair. Next came frail Helen with her purse held before her in both hands, red wig piled high as ever. Finally, Dad walked in, small, bald on top and gray on the sides, and dressed in an extra-large tee shirt that made him look like a child. He carried a worn backpack over one shoulder and a guitar case in the opposite hand. "Well how do?" Gil asked, and smacked my shoulder, sending me stumbling to the side. "Here's your father."

"I see that," I said, rubbing my shoulder.

Gil was a big man, a former soldier and nightclub bouncer. Our friendship was based on him playfully beating me up. Now and then he demonstrated his knowledge of "pressure points," dropping me to my knees with an easy press of his meaty fingers into my wrist, elbow or shoulder. "Helen," he said, "let's go downstairs and leave these men to talk." He winked at me, a gesture I didn't understand. Then they were gone. I couldn't imagine how they'd passed the six-hour drive home.

"Welcome back," I said. "Must feel good to be free."

"That it does," he said, glancing around the room, terra cotta tiled, with French doors that led to the small, stone-paved entranceway, lush with potted plants that gardeners cared for. The house was unfamiliar to my dad, having been purchased a few years after he'd run. The moment Gil bought a house, he'd put it up for sale. He saw this as a wise investment technique, selling at a greater price than he'd paid. Then he'd use the profit to buy a new house, this one as inflated as the one he'd just sold. I think he was simply restless, bored, looking for the answer, that great magical deal in the sky, the proverbial steal. "Not sure I'd call myself free at this point," Dad said, "but I'm getting there."

"I hear you," I said. "No one's really free, huh?"

"I was talking about parole."

"Ah. I see. You hungry?"

"I could eat."

"Steak sound good?"

"Why not?"

"Steak it is," I said, and felt like a rich man condescending to a pauper, though of course nothing in the house was mine. Technically, it was closer to his, when you considered inheritance. "You know Gil. He's always got a freezer full of meat."

"I do know Gil," Dad said, nodding thoughtfully. The fact was, my dad didn't try to hide his contempt for his step-father, in spite of the fortune Gil had spent trying to keep him out of prison. The more Gil gave, the less Dad liked him. My father had always resented his status as a rich kid. All the way back in elementary school, he'd told Helen not to pick him up after school in her shiny Cadillac. He wanted to skateboard home with his friends. As an adolescent, he'd once hitchhiked with his board from Corona del Mar to Doheny Beach. The man who picked him up offered him twenty dollars to pose shirtless for some snapshot. Dad, in his words, knew the guy was a pervert, but he didn't care. He let the creep take some pictures and accepted the money, though Helen would have given him a twenty without a thought. Dad didn't want to be a kid whose mother gave him money. He saw himself a scrappy survivor, who lived by his wits and the strength of his body. He wore his jeans until they fell apart, and then he patched them with spare fabric, needle, and thread. He always drove, and maintained, clunkers; he often slept in them, too. When the gas crisis of the 1970s hit, he converted his pickup to run on liquid propane. He was always waiting for the apocalypse, and probably hoping for it on some level—Swiss Army knife at the ready. And yet, when he found trouble—and he was always finding trouble—he ran back to his mother and step father, back to the cushioning money he'd been born into. He never forgave them for always being there for him, always rescuing him from his mistakes; they were his addiction, his weakness. Not that I understood this back then. His resentment toward his parents simply made me resent him.

We moved into the kitchen, an open space in the center of the floor, in view of the living room, with its wet bar and arched windows looking out at the ocean. I tossed two frozen ribeyes on the indoor grill. Though I craved a beer, I poured two glasses of water instead. For some reason, it seemed important to play at sobriety, for Dad's homecoming at least. As the steaks sizzled and spat, Dad took his glass of water into the high-ceilinged living room. He opened one of the French doors and let in a strong, salty breeze. "It's good to smell the ocean," he called from the shallow balcony overlooking Three Arch Bay.

"I bet."

Ten minutes later, I forked the steaks onto plates and trucked them to the table. "Soup's on," I said, a dorky phrase I'd gotten from Gil. Dad sat across from me, put his head down, his elbows out, and went at the meat like a beast. I was a fast eater myself, embarrassingly so if I didn't watch out, but I'd hardly chewed my first mouthful when Dad looked up from the clean plate, smiling sheepishly.

"Sorry," he said. "That's how you have to do it inside."

"I can imagine," I replied, picturing movie scenes of hundreds of inmates, segregated by color, eating tense meals, shoulder-to-shoulder, alert for shankings.

"I'm going to have to get used to the way things work out here."

"Must be strange," I said, chewing.

"Strange it is. Hey, you mind pointing the way to my room? I think I'll do a little reading and turn in. Been a long day. How about we catch up tomorrow?"

"You bet," I said, a little too eagerly.

He grabbed his stuff, and I showed him down the side stairway to the large deck outside the studio. I opened one of the glass doors, with its clanking wooden blinds. "There's a couch, no bed," I said, "but it has the best view in the house."

"I don't need a bed," he said. "Matter of fact, I think I'll sleep on the floor." He removed the blanket and sheets from the couch. "This carpet's thicker than most beds in the P.I."

"It was like that in Central America, too." I waited by the door for a response, but it didn't come. "Well, good night," I said, though the sun hadn't set.

The next morning I found him on the deck, playing guitar, cup of coffee on the glass-topped table. I nodded hello and leaned out over the rail. The sun was already breaking through the haze, and small waves plashed below. Three Arch Bay was a cove, a half-mile long, and we were on the southern end. It wasn't technically private, as no one could legally own the beach in California, but the access points were owned and gated. Even so, there was nothing stopping anyone from taking a boat in, or simply swimming around the points. I myself had once embarked upon a sea kayak tour of Laguna's so-called private beaches. Regardless, Three Arch was rarely crowded, and when it was, on the Fourth of July for example, it felt more like a private party than a mob scene. The water below was pale green-blue and clear to the sandy bottom for about fifty feet. Farther out, the water turned a deep, rich blue, like the sky an hour after sunset. A steep, rocky cliff to the south was home to hundreds of cormorants, which spent their days diving into the water after fish or resting in their cliff-side nests. Pelicans glided inches over the waves, looking to scoop a meal. They gathered on the rock out front of our house, sharing it with the ubiquitous gulls. On the northern end of the beach rose Turtle Rock, under which the ocean had bored three large tunnels, which gave Three Arch its name. The rock itself was fifty feet high and big enough to build a mansion on, surrounded by water except for a little piece that touched the beach. Rumor had it that someone was always about to build a house there, but of course, there would be no plausible way to get a car onto the little island, and the community would never let that happen in any event. McDonalds couldn't even get a franchise into Laguna, and every dive bar except one, an old gin mill beloved by various important Lagunites, had been run out of town.

The rocky beaches in and around Laguna were some of the most beautiful places I'd ever been, each with its own personality, its own vibe, as we say. And though it was a thriving resort, tourists rarely ventured beyond Main Beach. Sometimes I imagined renting one of the tiny studios on the winding, narrow roads along Laguna's hillsides, or a drafty old shack in Laguna Canyon, hunkering down with a crummy job I didn't care about and planting myself forever. One could do worse, and yet this just seemed too easy somehow. Wasn't there more to life than simply existing in a beautiful place? Maybe, maybe not.

"This guitar about saved my life inside," Dad said, tuning. "I got a lot better too. There aren't many benefits to prison, but spare time is one of them."

I pulled up a chair opposite him. He looked better today, very fit in shorts and a gray sweatshirt with the sleeves cut off at the shoulders. His muscles looked as firm as ever, and the forearms bulged with veins. I'd often marveled at these veins when I was a boy, fascinated, wondering if my arms would ever be like that. Now I knew the answer. No, they would not.

"You remember 'Friend of the Devil'?" I asked.

He laughed. "Oh, sure." He began, plucking and singing much faster than the recorded version, just as he always had when I was a boy, as if he were desperate to get the story out before that sheriff caught up to him.

I clapped when it was over. I wanted to tell him about Jerry Garcia, but he was still playing the guitar, eyes on the fret board, jazz riffs that may or may not have been a song, nodding to the rhythm. Ten minutes later he was still noodling, and I looked out at the ocean and wondered what to do with my day. The closest I'd come to finding a job was an interview scheduled for next week at The Ritz Carlton Hotel down PCH, where I'd applied to appease Gil. I wasn't spending much money here at Casa Three Arch, but I wasn't making anything either. I'd been hanging around in limbo, waiting for Dad, and now that he was here, I couldn't help feeling a little disappointed.

I sat there for a few minutes, waiting for an opportunity to take my leave, but before I could, he abruptly stopped playing and began to tell me about his "road dogs," prison code for best buddies, several guys his age, musicians he'd hung with in the yard. They'd sit in a circle playing and singing, and when some new kid came around hoping to join their crew, my father would look the newcomer in the eye and say, "Hey, I'm not in here for drugs."

"Yeah?" I asked, not sure what to make of this information.

"Just about everybody's in for drugs."

"Oh, I see," I said. "And you were in for something much worse."

I didn't care much for this brand of braggadocio, and what's more, I didn't want to hear about Dad's friends in prison, didn't want to know that he was wondering how they were, that he was planning to look them up when they got out, set up some kind of road dog reunion. Seemed to me he'd want to stay as far as possible from the people he'd met in that place.

"The worst thing about prison," he went on, "are the prisoners, the general population. Not the brightest bunch you'll meet."

"I believe that," I said, thinking of Ole and his ilk, who, once out, immediately began devising ways to get back in. Or so it seemed to me.

"Whenever anybody talked about some new scam they were going to pull once they got out, robbing a bank or some kind of credit card rip-off, I'd always remind them that we're not very good at being criminals. Otherwise, we wouldn't be in here."

I could tell by the rising, sarcastic tone of voice that he meant this to be a joke, so I laughed, but I didn't find the observation funny, true as it clearly was. I hated prison, the idea of it, the people in it, the people running it, the buildings and walls and showers and stories— everything— and I didn't want to talk about it or hear about it.

He strummed a loud, flamenco flourish.

"Did I ever tell you I used to be in a band?" I asked, to change the subject. It was one of the accomplishments I was most proud of, a punk-folk mutation that ultimately went nowhere, but we had played a few gigs, to some small acclaim.

"You're a drummer, right?"

"Used to be. We weren't bad. Only lasted about a year before I moved to San Francisco, but we made a demo tape."

Dad nodded his head, plucking out a little lead. "Why'd you give up music?"

"Ah." I brushed away the question with a sweep of my hand. "I wasn't that into it, wasn't that good. My buddy Richard was the real talent. He wrote all the songs, sang, played guitar. For me it was an excuse to party, to meet girls. I wanted to be a rock star, not a musician. Besides, I had to move away for college."

"Maybe we can start up a band ourselves one of these days. You know, balance all that studying you've been doing with something more visceral. Drums, surfing, something primal, body oriented. Inside, sometimes I'd worry about you a little, living in your head so much."

"Worry about me, huh?"

"Not as much as your brother."

"Well, I wasn't just living in my head. The city has its own kind of energy. Lot of creativity going on, plenty of action. Hey, you interested in hearing our demo? I've got a cassette upstairs."

Dad wasn't listening. He'd fallen into a little guitar solo, eyes closed, head wobbling from side to side. I slipped away, up the steps and into the garage, where I'd stashed the old surf board in a broom closet. I brought it down, and Dad hopped out of his seat.

"What have we here?" he asked, spinning it on its tail, examining it with professional brusqueness.

"I found it behind your wall."

"What a trip. I glassed this board myself. I could have used it in the P.I. We had some big days over the years."

"I thought you might be interested. I took it out in the water a few days ago."

"I can see. That's why it's waterlogged. One, two, three… Nine dings. It's seen better days, but I can fix it. Come on. Let's talk to the oldies."

I followed him up the steps and in through a side door. Helen looked up from the table where she sorted mail and wrote checks.

"Hello dear," she said. "Did you sleep well? I'm sorry we don't have a bed down there. I told Gil—"

"Slept great. Listen, I need some supplies. Resin, fiberglass, a heavy-duty blow dryer. Maybe some sheet plastic. Oh, and a wetsuit. Dad's sending me money, so I can pay you back." He was referring to his biological father, another relatively wealthy man, who lived in

Sacramento.

"Phooey," Helen said. "Gil! We need to go out."

We climbed into Gil's Lexus, and I recalled the many times I'd sat in the back seat of one of Gil and Helen's luxury cars over the course of my life, next to Ole as we headed to the mall, or the hair stylist, or even Disneyland. Over the years, Gil had driven Cadillacs, a Corvette, a second -hand Lamborghini, a couple of Jaguars, and now he swore by Lexus. "This is the greatest car ever built," he said, pulling out of the garage, today in a lime-green Hawaiian shirt and beige slacks. Every car he'd owned had been the greatest ever built. "Notice this screen here?" He pointed to a monitor in the console. "There's a camera located under the bumper so I can see what's behind when I back up."

"Why not just turn your head?" Dad asked.

"This is a hell of a car," Gil concluded. "You'll never see another like it." He turned the radio onto Helen's mariachi station.

We drove into Dana Point and parked in a strip mall outside a large surf and scuba shop. Dad led the way in, and I lagged behind, like a teenager ashamed to be seen with his family. "I need a full suit," Dad told the salesman. "Something warm. I'm too old for this cold water." And then he rattled off some specifications and brand names. Gil and Helen stood behind him like bodyguards.

"Give him the best," Gil said. "Nothing's too good for my family."

"You dive as well as surf?" the salesman asked, showing us to the racks. He was a gawky, mustachioed man in his thirties, tall and too skinny.

"Only for food," my father said, staring at the man as if challenging him to a fight.

"Let me know if I can help," the salesman said, and left.

"Why don't you pick something out?" Dad called to me as I edged away. I nodded my head and moved to the rack where they kept the spring suits, which were about half the price of the full suits but still quite expensive. This was yet another chance to profit from Gil's generosity. I never refused these opportunities, but I never sought them out either; I certainly didn't enjoy them. At such moments, I understood my father best, but then I'd forget the uncomfortable incident the moment it had passed, and nothing would be gained except some item I didn't have to pay for. The first suit I pulled off the rack had long sleeves and short legs. It was black with purple flanks, otherwise pretty much like all the others.

"Are you going to surf with your father?" Helen asked, having appeared at my side like a fairytale crone and speaking in the cartoon voice she usually reserved for small children. The prospect of me surfing delighted and amused her.

"Yes," I said, and locked myself in the changing room. The wetsuit seemed to fit, but I looked ridiculous in the mirror, like a guy in a superhero costume. I changed back into street clothes and walked out with the wetsuit draped over my shoulder. "I'll take it," I announced.

My father stood before a mirror, barefoot in the wetsuit. He suddenly dipped into a crouch, rose and pulled hard at the sleeves, checking elasticity or thickness or whatever. He threw his arms around, twisting like a hula-hooper until finally he stood still and nodded to the mirror. I thought he might try a few karate kicks, but apparently he was satisfied. "Seems a little thin for winter," he said, "but I'll give it a try."

"It's the best we've got," the salesman ventured. "We stand by the quality."

"We'll see."

"Anything else?" Gil asked, and Dad threw in a few sticks of wax. Out came the American Express card, and we piled into the Lexus with our booty. "Thanks, Grandpa," I said as we pulled onto the highway.

"Yeah, thanks," Dad added.

"No need to thank me. That's the only reason I make money to begin with, to take care of you kids. How about some lunch?"

We cut inland to Capistrano and stopped at a little Mexican joint. As we ate, Gil slipped a dollar bill to each of the three busboys, and after the meal he barged into the kitchen to compliment the chef. "Hola amigo," he said, and stuck something into the pocket of his cook's smock. "Muchas gracias."

"*A usted*," the baffled man replied.

"Oh, Gil," Helen said, shaking her head when he returned to the table. "Did you give him a five-dollar tip? My word. You know he has a wage, don't you?" Gil paid the bill, and we got into the Lexus. Helen turned to face my dad and me over the back seat. "Did I ever tell you about our first date?"

Dad closed his eyes and laid his head back against the rest.

"Gil ordered an entire chateaubriand, just for himself! The waiter couldn't believe it. He ate the whole thing."

"I was hungry," Gil said, and turned up the mariachis.

At ten that night, the phone rang as I lay in bed reading. I immediately recognized the sweet, accented way she said my name. I never thought I'd hear from Gaby again; her family had no phone, and couldn't afford a call like this even if they did. She explained that she'd found a free line, pirated into the home of some cousin or other. I chose to believe this story. I was lonely and had missed her.

She called again the next night, and by the end of the week, I'd begun to anticipate our daily talks. Sometimes we talked about sex, the things we'd done and liked to do, the things we missed and wanted to do right now. Other times, we fantasized about building a life together again, but this time better in some undefined way. I shared my latest dream of moving to Argentina, where I'd teach English and write novels. Maybe I could swing by and pick her up on the way, as if Argentina were the next town over and Gaby lived down the block. Gaby, in turn, spoke of coming up north to join me here. You'd love it, I told her. It's even prettier than Vallarta.

I realized that continuing this impossible affair over the phone wasn't exactly healthy, but I liked dreaming with her in Spanish, and I didn't want to wake from it. The fact was, I hadn't managed to reenter the Laguna social scene the way I'd hoped. It seemed my time in Mexico had marked me somehow, like sandpaper over veneer, and I never felt comfortable in Laguna's gleaming and pricy hot spots; I'd sit at a bar or table, even among old friends, imagining that everyone was looking me over and finding me unsatisfactory. The alienation I'd experienced in Vallarta among tourists had somehow followed me here, but instead of tourists, it was Americans in general I'd been cut off from. Alone and self -conscious in some flashing nightclub or chic martini bar full of beautiful women and conspicuously wealthy men, I might as well have been back in Solter's class, hiding in the corner, still that same weirdo afraid of the cool kids.

Over the next weeks, Dad transformed half the garage into what he called a ding-repair shop, having installed a wall of plastic sheeting down the center to keep the dust off the Lexus, or perhaps to stake out his territory. So far he was his only customer, but he planned to turn the shop into a little business. Meanwhile, my spring suit hung unused in the closet, until Dad caught me eating cereal one morning, and invited me to hit a surf shop for some gear and head to The Cove.

I agreed. The Frog House was something of a landmark, an old board shop where Dad had often taken me when I was a kid. I pulled the tags off the spring suit while Dad tied the repaired gun to the roof racks of the used Toyota wagon his father had paid for. We hopped in and drove up the coast. "Here you go," Dad said, and passed me a crisp hundred dollar bill. "Les sent me some money," he explained. "I figured I'd give you a cut, you being my son and all. We're in this together, seems to me."

I thanked him and slipped the bill into the wax pocket of my trunks. "It'll go to my travel fund."

The Frog House had a wholly different atmosphere from the Dana Point shop. The logo was fearsome rather than matter-of-fact, an angry monster frog with a wide open mouth that contained a surfer in a mammoth tube. The shop itself was crammed to the ceiling with boards and gear. They didn't sell much beachwear, or in any other way cater to tourists. Only a couple of shaggy-looking boys pawed boards they'd later beg their parents to buy, small things these days, with multiple fins and supersonic jutting lines. Dad shook hands with the crusty, bearded fellow working the counter. "Nice to see you back in the world," the guy said in a gravelly smoker's voice. Dad introduced me as his son. "I remember you when you came up to my knee," the man said. I used to get a lot of that before Dad got busted. "What are you looking for?"

"We're thinking about setting him up with a decent sponge," Dad said.

"Well, we got sponges," the salesman replied.

These body boards started at a hundred dollars. The ones in the beach stores sold for around thirty. I didn't recognize the brands, endorsed by riders I also didn't recognize, so I chose a board that looked about right, in an understated green color, no flashy design features, just a big X on the deck. The tag boasted of a space-age mesh fiber for stiffness, and the price hung around the middle of the pack. I grabbed some fins, not the most popular brand, which were a distinctive blue and yellow and easily recognizable on the beach, but a newer sort I'd seen around a few times, black, with no-nonsense, triangular geometry. I was just guessing, of course, but I tried to act as if I knew what I wanted.

So, I thought as Dad paid, I was going to be a sponger. Sponging was certainly the lowest-ranking wave sport, even worse than skim boarding, but who cared, after all? I'd be hanging with an old-time local, so I wasn't worried about getting rousted. And, besides, after a bit of practice on the sponge, I'd work my way up to a real board. I'd be surfing in no time.

We got into the car and drove down PCH, through an industrial zone created before the value of beachfront property was fully anticipated. "You mind if I ask how you got manslaughter instead of murder?" The question had been on my mind.

"Well," he said, thinking it over. "I have to hand it to Gil. He really came through. Not just once but twice. He got me out on bail, and paid a lot of money for a good lawyer. In the end, I got justice. If you don't have money in this country, you've got no chance. Everybody deserves a lawyer like my guy."

"But why manslaughter? Doesn't that mean it was an accident?"

"Not exactly. The whole legal thing is trippy, but the technicalities don't matter as much as you think. It's more primitive than that. My lawyer was a storyteller, basically. Back in the caveman days, he'd have been the one at the fire that got a free meal just to tell everybody how the hunt went, or how it was last year or whatever. He talked a lot about me and Duke, believe it or not. You remember Duke?"

"Of course."

Duke, a black-and-white husky, had appeared one day on the edge of the Anza property, after my mom, Ole, and I had moved out and Dad took our place. Dad, an animal lover, had coaxed him forward, and after some hesitation, the dog came limping up, one of his front legs dangling from some bloody tendons. Dad rushed him an hour's drive to the nearest vet, who saved his life by amputating the leg. "Shotgun blast," the vet had said. "Some ranchers probably caught him chasing livestock."

"I remember when I first called him to the cabin," Dad said. "He stood there, half in the bushes, wondering whether or not to trust this guy. I figure he either saw something he liked, or he just didn't have any other options at that point. The doc said the wound was three days old. That means Duke was fighting off coyotes all that time. Pretty tough dog."

Duke and my father were inseparable after that, and I'd never met a dog I liked as much. They were known up and down the coast, the surfer and his three-legged husky.

"What did Duke have to do with the case?" I asked. We were passing a field of oil derricks, big, greasy rocking horses up on the hills overlooking the ocean. A pipe rose from the earth among the derricks, topped by a flame that never went out.

"The strategy was to show the jury that I was an okay guy," Dad said, "just a peace-loving, dog-loving surfer who really fucked up. Pretty much the truth. The prosecutor was this little angry man, a total cop all the way. He even had that cop mustache. I remember how he'd crack this tiny smile after he'd put some witness down. When the time came to decide, the jury didn't want to put me away for the rest of my life. They liked my guy's story better than the other guy's story."

We left the oil fields and entered the heart of Newport. Up on an inland hill sat the hospital where I was originally supposed to have been born. Gil and Helen and my mother's father had organized the birth, but then my father learned the doctor insisted on delivering me through c-section, claiming that my mother would die if she tried to birth me naturally. Dad and Mom refused to go along with this, but the doctor wouldn't budge. Finally, at the zero hour, Dad checked Mom out of the hospital, and took her home to their one-bedroom apartment in Costa Mesa, leaving the parents to battle it out with each other and the doctor. I entered the world at two-o'clock in the morning, under the supervision of the "manager" of Dad's surf rock band, a middle-aged former doctor who'd lost his license and who liked to hang out with teenagers. I always pictured him doling out pills on the beach. Dad was eighteen, Mom nineteen.

"Sometimes," Dad ruminated, stuck in the permanent Newport traffic, "I wonder if I was meant to do what I did. You know what I mean? It was like I was possessed, doing the work of someone or something else. Like the guy had to be stopped, and I was the one chosen for the mission."

I made a sound, a brief exhalation, not quite a raspberry.

Dad looked over. "Or maybe that's bullshit," he said, smiling, embarrassed.

"No opinion," I said, but I did have an opinion. This kind of talk was absolutely bullshit, and it pissed me off that my father was still trying to dodge responsibility for his actions, even after all these years. I could accept that he didn't like to work—I didn't either—and that he was going to live off his parents his whole life, that he felt sorry for himself in comparison to the trust-fund kids he'd grown up with. But why, I wondered, couldn't he simply admit he'd done wrong and say he was sorry, sorry for killing Barkley and leaving everyone else to clean up the mess, sorry for blowing through so much of Gil and Helen's fortune that there wasn't enough left to help Ole with rehab and lawyers or help me pay for college, sorry that he'd left his young and broke family when they got in the way of his surfing and dope dealing? But no. Instead of owning up to his failures and asking forgiveness, he was trying to con me, and himself, into viewing him as some kind of cosmic player, righting the wrongs of the universe. But I, a coward when it came to anything that really mattered, didn't tell him any of this. I was tired of talking about it, and wished I'd never brought up the murder in the first place.

We pulled into Crystal Cove State Park, where Dad was already on a first-name basis with the kiosk ranger. "This used to be all dirt," he said, navigating along a winding system of blacktop roads to the northernmost parking lot. The other times I'd visited The Cove, we'd walked from Cameo Shores, where my grandparents had lived then, along a dusty footpath through chest-high, brown grass. Now the paths were paved and marked with signs that described the flora and fauna native to the area. I walked with the body board under my arm, spring suit draped over and fins in my free hand. For all the changes, the place smelled as I remembered it, of hot, dusty sandstone, and, descending new concrete steps down to the beach, rotting kelp. The Cove took up the northern end of the beach, where sand and water butted up against the large rocky point, fist-shaped and striated. A dark, dripping cave gaped in the middle of the fist. To the south, the beach was wide and empty of people, stretching a good mile until it curved inland out of sight. Piles of kelp, buzzing with insects, lay about the sand like strewn laundry.

The Cove owed its success to three main factors. It was rocky and irregular, "hairy" to the novice or first-time visitor. Dripping black rocks bristling with spiky mussels seemed to jump from the water in front of breaking waves, and the ocean all around boiled and sloshed over reefs. It was also a State Park, which cost five dollars to enter. Finally, the wave just wasn't that great. All of this combined to keep most surfers away, so we had the place to ourselves, even after all these years.

We paddled out, over the dark reefs and small spots of bright sand. The short, stubby board was a lot easier to handle than the slippery gun, and I felt confident on the board and warm in my new suit. We got outside and I risked sitting up on the board. I found that, with the aid of the fins below, I could keep my balance with minimum effort.

"It's still The Cove," Dad said.

"Yeah, but the houses are coming," I said, pointing to what used to be brown hills, now covered by red-tiled roofs.

"There's always Mexico," Dad replied. He'd been born in Mexico City and so enjoyed dual citizenship. Helen had been something of an adventuress in her youth. She'd fled Amarillo, Texas and her tyrannical father for Hollywood, where she'd eked a living as a department store model. At one point, she'd traveled with her bold sister deep into Mexico, where she met Les, her first husband and my father's father. A former WWII pilot, Les ran a small airline in the Mexican capital. This meant Dad could own property in Mexico, whereas non-citizens could only lease. "One of these days when I get some money," he said, "I'd like to buy a place in Baja, a surf rancho where you and your brother can run when things get weird up here."

"Yeah? Where in Baja?"

"I figure down south, where the water is warm. I got to admit, I don't much like the cold water around here. It's okay when you're young, but I got used to things in the P.I."

"Sounds like a good idea," I said, excited in spite of my skepticism. My father had been talking this way since I could remember, and nothing ever came of his big schemes. But, I told myself, an inheritance could make a big difference.

"All I need is a plot of beach with access to fresh water. I could rent boards and palapa space. Maybe give some lessons. You got these surf camps where people send their kids to get them out of their hair for the summer. I'm even thinking about building some horse stables. Surf and horses. I don't know. Just seems to go together. All the women I've dug, like your mother, were into horses."

I could see it, the confluence of desert and ocean, a place to escape to, maybe even a place to stay. I'd surf when I wasn't helping out with the laid-back tourist operation, sleep in a hammock. Eventually I'd join forces with a beautiful local woman, or perhaps a free-spirited traveler, a surfer girl happening by. Maybe I'd reunite with Gaby, older now, and wiser. I'd add a little bar and restaurant to the camp. Nothing fancy. Just drinks and whatever the fishermen brought in from the sea. Bar with a thatch roof. Four or five tables. Real margaritas with fresh lime and good tequila. That and Pacifico beer. Take it or leave it. The menu? Fish tacos. I bet we'd attract some local mariachis, to hang around and play for tips.

"I talked to Rick about it," Dad said, absently paddling to keep the board facing the horizon. Rick was one of Dad's old friends, a real good guy. "He's got a trust fund, and I'm trying to strike a deal. He'll pay for the property, and I'll take care of the legal issues."

"Is he interested?"

"I don't see why not."

I saw why not, but decided not to press. I preferred to believe in Dad this time.

"You got this one?" he asked, pointing to a bump on the horizon. I kicked toward it. As it rose, I turned and paddled, but it passed under me and broke where I'd originally been positioned. "You need to set up right on the boils," Dad said. "That tells you where it'll break. Like this," he said, and turned as the second wave of the set approached. He took off with a graceful slide, rode for a moment in a pushup position, and then hopped easily to his feet. The wave moved beyond me, and I only saw him from the shoulders up, a head gliding along the cresting lip. A third wave drew near, and I forced myself to wait for it in the churning boil, though I didn't like the looks of jagged rock below and the water bubbling around me. The wave began to break before it reached me, and the foam enveloped me and pushed me toward the shore. I angled the board to the right, trying to maneuver out of the foam and into the unbroken face, but the board didn't seem to be working right. Instead of riding along the face, as was supposed to happen, I simply bumped forward, sideways in the foam.

"I've never sponged," Dad said when I got back out, "but the guys I've seen really crank up on the rail to get the thing to turn."

"Uh-huh," I said, a little dispirited. "I'll get it next time."

We sat for a while in silence, and then Dad asked if I talked to my mom much.

"Now and then."

"She happy with things?"

"I guess."

Dad was probably wondering if she felt she'd made the right decision to go straight, relatively, instead of remaining on the path they'd started together. Did she regret the road not taken? I thought it was more likely she regretted following Dad in the first place, turning Ole and I loose in the desert like wild animals, ignoring health and money until it had been almost too late. But I didn't tell Dad this. It would have felt like a betrayal of her.

I first learned about Mom's illness in Redlands, though it started way back in Anza. Back then, she'd assumed the bloody stools, cramps, and weakness was cancer, but instead of consulting a doctor, she read a book on natural remedies. None of the herbs and such worked, of course, and finally she got so sick, while pregnant with my half brother, Jeremy, that she had to go to a hospital. The doctor diagnosed her with Crohn's disease, and put her on powerful steroids, drugs that were almost as hard on her body as the disease. She'd been on them ever since, and they'd been taking a toll. Luckily, she'd gotten a job at The City of Hope as a secretary, so when the time came to have her colon removed, which I figured was inevitable but which she insisted wasn't, she'd have insurance. Ralph worked there, too, as a locksmith. They owned a tract home in Rancho Cucamonga, and they skydived for weekend thrills. Somewhere along the line, they'd become disillusioned with the church, and now they lived secular, normal lives—if you didn't count the skydiving. I liked to believe Mom was happy, at least content, and I thought that probably she was.

"I hear they put your brother in the S.H.U. program," Dad said. "Solitary confinement all day, every day. Amnesty International calls it torture."

"Great," I said.

"I was lucky to go in at my age. Old men aren't expected to fight anymore, but the young guys are front-line soldiers in the race wars. Ole's definitely bought into the whole prison order."

I'd largely given up hope that Ole would ever change, but it was still a knife in the gut every time he got busted, or had extra time tacked on for fighting, or when he ended up in the prison hospital for hepatitis, or it came to light that he'd fathered a little girl who was now growing up out in the desert without a dad. I'd avoid calling my mother for months sometimes, because she was usually the one to give me the latest bad news. I didn't want to hear about it anymore.

I especially hated to consider my own role in Ole's string of bad decisions. The fact was, Ole began his life as an outlaw by following my example. He'd been watching me carefully after Dad split, looking for clues I guess, looking for an example of how to be. When I'd gotten into my Spicoli transformation, I could see that Ole thought I was cool. Once I even allowed him a little hit of a roach I'd saved from school. I guess neither of us knew what we were doing; neither of us understood that this was all just a game to me, as much a role for me as it had been for Sean Penn. But for Ole, crime became the real thing, his calling. By the time any of us realized what was happening, Ole was already too far gone, already stuck deep in a California juvenile offender system that would later be excoriated by various courts and organizations for its incompetence and cruelty, not only failing to rehabilitate prisoners but demonstrably harming them.

Why him, I sometimes wondered, and not me? Well, he'd gotten into dope and crime much younger than I had, and he also seemed to be more prone to physical addiction. But the differences went deeper than this. I'd always been a pretender, what we used to call a poser. Ole was sincere. He was also sweeter than I was, more sensitive, more empathetic. When we were kids, he never forgot Mom's birthday, unlike me. Once, when I was in high school and Ole junior high, Mom asked us to do the dishes, and when we finished, Ole explained how happy it made Mom if we simply wiped the water off the counter. I'd never have thought of that in a million years.

I sat on the board, brooding on Mom, physically ill and commuting three hours a day in traffic, living in a tract home worth less than she owed on it; and on Ole, slowly going crazy in a windowless, featureless room, alone all day and all night. A wave rose behind me and I caught it, but again I couldn't figure out how to turn the board. I tried, with no improvement, for an hour more, until I finally gave up and rode foam to the shore, where I stood and promptly plunged face first onto the damp sand, tripping over the fins on my feet. Enough, I thought, rolling onto my back and yanking off the fins. I flung them onto the beach, and ran after my frolicking board before the surf carried it away. I grabbed it and stomped up the beach, to the old log at the base of the cliff where Dad's buddies used to smoke dope and wait for the next session. I'd imagined surfing so often and for so long that it seemed as if I'd been doing it, but I hadn't been doing it, and now I understood that I couldn't; I did not have the ability. Dad was a surfer. He grew up at the beach. I grew up in the desert and played baseball. The facts were the facts.

I'd never wanted it this way, but that's how it was. We were different. He woke early, I slept in. He smoked pot, I drank beer. He was into nature, I liked cities. We had nothing in common, nothing to talk about. Fine. We'd tried. That's life. Now it was over, the whole surfing thing, the whole father-son thing. No big tragedy. Shaking with cold and rage and a deep, sickening disappointment, I peeled off the wetsuit, yanked my trunks on, and sat on the log to watch my father surf, as I'd done, on that very same piece of driftwood, so often as a child.

Chapter Twelve

The Ritz

Gil looked over my shoulder as I fried onions and mushrooms for another scrambled "eggstravaganza," as we called these customary breakfasts. By default, we'd been spending a lot of time together. Helen was always gone, shopping, brunching, playing bridge, or off to the library for another stack of detective books. She'd long ago learned how to keep busy. Gil, since retiring, had not yet mastered that skill. Often, he lounged around in his white briefs all day, though today he'd managed to dress, which meant a run to the grocery store once Helen returned with the car. Dad also stayed away from home most of the time. He and Gil avoided each other unless one of them felt like picking a fight. I'd fallen into the role of Gil's sidekick, a life focused on food. Gil bought it, I cooked it, and together we ate it, watching television in the den and planning the next meal. "You want to grab a couple of plates?" I asked Gil, and poured the whipped eggs into the pan.

"You've got a real talent, son," Gil said, sliding the plates onto the cutting board island. I flipped the potatoes to show off a little.

"Thanks," I said, though I felt an extra edge on Gil's compliment. Everything he said these days seemed designed, subtly or blatantly, to drive me toward a vocation. He'd given up trying to talk me into joining the military, but now he liked to imagine me rising through the ranks of the food service industry, just as he'd done in produce distribution. He thought I'd make a great restaurant manager someday.

The phone rang as I knocked the eggs about with a wooden spoon. Gil answered the line in the kitchen. "Yello," he said. "Sure. One moment."

"It's for you," he whispered, hand over the mouth piece. "The Ritz Carlton." This wasn't a big surprise. The Ritz had interviewed me three times recently, and administered three corresponding tests: psychological, skills, and drugs. All to serve food to rich people.

I turned off the burner. Gil stood by as a man named Brad from Human Resources offered me a position as a server at the Terrace Café, the Ritz's version of a casual restaurant.

"Well?" Gil said after I'd hung up.

"I got the job."

"Oh, boy. That's great young man." His pride touched and depressed me. "That's quite an operation they've got there," he said. He'd recently bought a new set of eyeglasses, ornate gold frames with chains looping down around jowls that shook when he spoke. He was getting old, and I realized that I, in my way, was too. "I'll tell you," he said, "you'd be a fool to let this one go."

"Sure," I said, thinking, Who knows? Maybe he was right. So far I'd left San Francisco, and now Mexico; I'd left good friends and lovers. One of these days I was going to have to stick with something, someone, somewhere. "I'd better rescue breakfast," I said.

◆

What did one wear to an employee orientation at a five-star hotel? I'd never had that particular experience, so I chose a thrift-store suit of worsted wool (whatever that was) and my pale-yellow guayabera worn with the collar out over the coat lapels, finished off with Chuck Taylor high-tops. I had no car, so I rode an old ten-speed bike that had been in the garage as long as I remembered, three miles on PCH, half downhill and half back up as cars whizzed by at sixty miles and hour. This was early December, a day that was proving unusually hot. I arrived damp with sweat, soaked around my collar and under my arms. I felt a trickle down the center of my back as I locked the bike to a tree wrapped in Christmas lights.

A manager named Heather met us in the employee parking lot. She was a willowy woman in her twenties, with a washed-out, plain face and a mane of brown curls. She wore a long dress covered in tiny flowers, and she moved and spoke very slowly, as if afraid of startling or confusing us. My fellow new hires, about fifteen of them, weren't wearing suits. They were the kids I'd see at the Mission Viejo Mall, normal boys and girls in polo shirts tucked into pleated pants, short dresses or Capri pants and bright tops, all quite casual and easy to miss. They seemed pointedly to not notice me, and I stood alone about five feet from the rest of the bunch. A double-dose of sweat—part nerves, part heat—tracked down my face and continued to collect in my shirt. I mopped my brow with a worsted wool sleeve and wiped my hands on my thighs. Heather showed us into the employee entrance, a tunnel behind the hotel that reminded me of the secret entrance to the Bat Cave. The sweat mercifully began to dry in the subterranean air.

The walls echoed with footsteps and distant voices. Heather pointed out the locker rooms, where we'd change into our uniforms and shower. Was it my imagination or had she directed the word "shower" toward me? It was true that I was beginning to stink. The suit had been a mistake, clearly, and the polyester blend shirt wasn't helping matters. We climbed stairs and entered a kitchen unlike any I'd seen, something like Vulcan's workshop. Later we emerged from the kitchen into the stuffy elegance the guests came for, and Heather paused in an intersection in the hall, tricked out in paisley carpet, an antique mirror, a seascape painting from another century, and an ornate card table, all lit by a blazing chandelier. "Just to orient you," Heather said, "since this is an orientation…" She paused so a few of us could laugh. "In this direction is the Terrace Café," she explained, extending a bony finger. "Registration's down this hall, and over there's a little convenience store. It's for guests of course, but you can shop there too, in case you need something, like deodorant," she said, raising at eyebrow at me, "because it's very important to use deodorant."

Wait a minute, I wanted to protest. I don't usually smell like this! But when you stink, you stink, and I just had to stand there and take it.

Gil was waiting when I got home. "Well, how'd it go, Tiger?"

"Fine," I said.

"Tell me more."

"You're right. It's quite an operation."

"Well, how about the Christmas display? You know, they're world famous for their lights."

"I didn't see any lights," I said. "You mind if I get out of this suit?"

From then on, I rode to work in shorts. I'd shower with the rest of the help and don the olive slacks and paisley vest combo that matched the carpet. The first two weeks I had to "shadow" Francisco, a stocky man with a big head, pushing sixty. He introduced me to his "guests" and explained that I was training. "Oh, isn't that nice," the friendlier ones would say, and I'd smile like a halfwit. Most of my time was spent doing Francisco's prep work, which was double that of other restaurants I'd worked for. Why use one fork when you can manage to go through three over the course of lunch?

During training, I collected no tips, and every couple of days, all the servers were required to attend a meeting that apparently had nothing to do with us. The term "Total Quality Management" was in constant use, and even after five meetings I had no idea what it meant. Once I asked Heather for a definition, and she smiled euphorically. "It's hard to say," she said. "That's what's so great about it. It means so much you can't explain it. More like a feeling, or a way of life, than a set of rules."

"Like post modernism," I said, putting my college education to good use.

Heather frowned, as if thinking this over. "Yes, a lot like that," she finally said, and walked away.

Paying my dues, I told myself. When I finally got my own tables, the money would start pouring in. But then, the week of Christmas, I was turned loose, and the money didn't pour in. I made on average a little less than I'd made at Lori's Diner, while working much harder and having to kiss more ass.

"I've been meaning to talk to you," Heather said one morning.

"Talk away," I replied.

"Uh-huh." She cleared her throat. "I see on your resume that you have a degree in English."

"Yes. I am a Bachelor of English, according to the good people of— "

"—Well, I'd like you to take a look at this." She handed me a piece of paper. "You can use the computer in my office." She began to walk away. "Come on," she said, turning.

"What about my section?" I asked, following.

"Francisco will watch your tables until you're done."

"I assume he'll also watch my tips."

"Hey." She opened the door into a windowless office. "We're a team here."

"Of course. Yes. Just kidding."

I sat at an exceedingly neat desk and tried to decipher Heather's prose. To even understand the basic purpose behind the memo was no easy task.

"I hate writing," she bragged from the doorway.

"I can see that," I responded, and began to type.

When the memo had been rewritten to Heather's satisfaction, I was allowed to return to my section. My reward for helping her plagiarize me was that I had to write all of her memos from then on, for which I was given neither credit nor remuneration. Francisco, on the other hand, was making out like a bandit.

The holidays passed, and I worked up a potent disdain for the hotel. Sure, if I stayed with the Ritz for life, like old Francisco, I'd eventually end up making something approaching a legitimate salary, or maybe I'd even sell my soul like Heather for a regular paycheck. Francisco told me that she'd been a lowly hostess only a week before I'd been hired. Just like that, she'd gone from nobody anyone knew to somebody everyone hated. But you had to commit to the company to get at the money. Mercenaries—the standard at most restaurants—weren't appreciated at the Ritz, even if they were good. In the past, I'd always risen quickly up the ranks, mainly because I was fast and aggressive on the floor. I was also kind of a jerk, now that I thought about it, poaching other waiters' tables when they fell behind, instead of helping them. But that's how it went in the restaurant business as I knew it, survival of the fittest. Mr. Solter had been trying to tell us this all along.

But here at the Ritz, loyalty trumped ability; sucking up was the key to advancement. I wasn't going to thrive in this environment, but then, I didn't have to thrive. Without quite realizing it, I'd already decided to move on again. Mexico, which had seemed like a failure upon my return, now appeared as another training session, a warm-up for the real thing. Dreamy talks with Gaby about Argentina had begun to shape into something firmer, something approaching a plan. I'd always wanted to see Buenos Aires, a big, hip city, far from home but not so poor as Mexico and Central America, the kind of place an enterprising gringo could flourish. Whenever confronted by the usual Ritz indignities, I'd imagine myself at a sidewalk café, scribbling some future masterpiece onto a notebook, sipping espresso and watching a parade of beautiful women stroll by, all fascinated by the gringo writer. The Ritz couldn't hurt me; I was already gone.

Around this time, I began to body board with a coworker at a nearby break called Aliso, a very different wave from The Cove's. The bottom of

Aliso—sandy shore break—went from very deep, to very shallow, very quickly. This meant that waves reared up suddenly and curled over from top to bottom. The ride was too short and abrupt for surf boards, so spongers and skimboarders owned the place. For whatever reason, fear of death probably, I figured out how to steer the board right away. Dad had been right. The trick was to really crank up on the rail, use the board more as a tool than a vehicle.

The waves happened to be larger than usual that winter, a result of the "El Niño" conditions everybody was talking about. Aliso, a public beach featuring a pier shaped like a tennis racket, was always ride-able, usually big, sometimes huge. Twenty-foot faces weren't unheard of, thick waves that bashed the shore with what seemed like anger.

After a few weeks, I got to know Aliso like you can know a person. Usually you can predict what they'll do. I'd take off just south of the pier and slide into the barrel, right shoulder skimming the face while a traveling waterfall crashed to the left. You could fit a dining room table in some of those barrels, hang a chandelier from the ceiling. Inside, a big intimate sound surrounded me, the sound of a shell to the ear but now I was in the shell. After a session, we'd rest in the sand, not bothering with towels, until we got hot and itchy and dove back into the water.

My buddy and I explored other breaks too, including the famous neck-breaker called The Wedge. I didn't know any tricks—no barrel rolls, spins, or drop knee riding—but I held my own and took my place in the lineup without shame. I could see how someone might not mind a crummy job with these waves waiting at the end of every shift.

"Can I see you in my office," Heather asked one day. I'd just clocked in for a rare lunch shift, filling in for Francisco. He'd taken a week off to visit family in Mexico, and I stood to make some money in his absence.

"Sure," I said, a little surprised. Heather had dispensed with asking if I'd write her memos. They'd just appear in my employee mailbox, along with the key to her office. She led the way, had me sit in the guest chair, and she closed the door. She handed me a paper. "This is your copy of a written warning."

"Oh?" I asked, and read what amounted to a description of a customer complaint. One day during a slow brunch, my body boarding colleague and I had begun to horse around, waging a battle by launching champagne corks into each other's server stations, like catapulting stones over enemy walls. One of my errant corks had landed on a table. It had done no harm, but at those prices, customers didn't like to see the help goofing off. I pictured the uptight old lady who'd complained, her wrinkles and harsh perfume masking the scent of decay. I hated her, and the company that catered to her whims. "Who'd you get to write it?" I asked.

She cleared her throat. "What's our motto?"

"Hmm. Let me think. Wait. I've got it. 'Servants groveling before the rich.'"

"Where's your card?"

While on duty, we were required to carry a laminated business card inscribed with the motto: *Ladies and gentlemen serving ladies and gentlemen.* The card was in my locker. I'd kept it on me for the first few weeks, but had eventually fallen out of the habit. I opened my wallet and tried to hand Heather a bar napkin with a phone number on it.

She sighed and blew a piece of hair that had fallen over her face. "Listen, do you want to work here?"

Instead of answering, I read the entire warning. It moved from a description of the incident to a general conclusion that, while I'd started well enough, I'd developed a lax attitude of late. It seemed I'd lost, the author riffed, "the eye of the tiger." It was an old story. No, I did not want to work here, but I needed the money.

"It's easy for you," Heather said in a voice I'd not heard before. Usually she sounded like a recording, but now she was exasperated, fed up. "You come in here, too good to follow the rules, thinking everything is stupid.

You'll hang around for a while, then quit, or get fired, and then you'll go on and get another job or do whatever you're going to do. But I need this job. I've got a son."

I noticed no wedding ring.

"The reason I'm writing you up is that you're causing problems. I appreciate that you help me with memos, okay? But customer complaints will get me fired. And if I'm fired, or demoted back to hostess, I won't be able to pay rent, and I'll have to move back into my mom's place, and my mom's a royal bitch. Nobody's forcing you to work here, you know. You can leave anytime you want. And if you screw up again, you'll be gone. That's what that little piece of paper means. Any questions?"

I folded the paper and put it in my pocket. "I hear you," I said, feeling childish and a little ashamed. "I'll behave. You have any extra motto cards?"

She took one from a drawer and I placed it in my vest pocket.

"'Ladies and gentlemen serving ladies and gentlemen,'" I said. "I remembered. I was just messing with you."

"I'd appreciate it if you'd stop messing with me."

"Agreed. But I'd also appreciate it if I didn't have to lose what little tip money I make writing memos."

She thought for a moment. "I'll write a letter of commendation to go in your file along with this warning. I'll let everyone know how valuable you've been, beyond your usual duties. That's the best I can do. Stations and shifts are assigned by seniority. I have no control of that. Klaus himself told me to make you write the memos."

Ah yes, Klaus, assistant to Davidson, the F. & B. Director. Heather had no real power, of course. She was paid to take the heat and fill out forms. The nice letter wasn't going to help me any—especially if she wrote it herself!—but the gesture was something. I shook Heather's hand and walked out of her office.

That evening, newly inspired to make something happen in my life, I took a bus to the library at Saddleback Community College. Soon I was leafing through a thick book that listed and ranked graduate programs throughout the U.S. I found a section devoted to Master of Fine Arts degrees in writing. I'd been jotting stories since high school, mostly in secret. It was a frustrating hobby in that hardly anyone ever read what I wrote, and those who did never seemed to get what I was trying to say. I had no real idea how to become an author, appealing as the idea was. A book called *The Writer's Market* shed little light on the subject, but I understood that if they accepted you into one of these M.F.A. programs, they'd let you teach freshman college courses in exchange for free tuition, plus a few bucks in your pocket. I didn't believe that more classes would make me a better writer—experience, such as Ernest Hemingway's real-life adventures, is what made writers—but I pictured myself holding forth in front of a class of freshmen, writing cryptic and crucial terms on the board and underlining them for emphasis, speaking to students who actually understood the English language. Why not? Besides, I'd liked college, and had come to miss the order it imposed, the constant beginning, middle, and end of the semester calendar, the lawns and trees and cheerful, innocent kids sitting around in the sun, waiting to inherit the world. I wasn't one of them, but I liked them and could easily fake it. So I drew up a list of ten universities whose deadlines hadn't already passed, all in distant metropolises. I paid no attention to rankings. I'd never heard of any of the teachers, and it didn't occur to me to hunt down their works. I just imagined living in New York, or Boston, or Atlanta, Miami, New Orleans, somewhere far-away and teeming.

Over the next days, however, the actual applications dampened my fire. What seemed like meaningless paperwork irritated me, as did the legalese prose. This irritation slipped into my materials as sarcasm, subtle mockery of the questions and requirements I found most threatening. I filled out forms hastily, aiming for wit and literary flourishes over substance. I completed two applications and sent them straight away, one to New

York City and the other to Atlanta, each with a separate writing sample. Atlanta got the story I'd written in Guatemala, about the gringo who wanted to become an ayudante. I sent a new story to New York, a postmodern, absurdly comic series of vignettes, cleverly and subtly connected.

Both works were first drafts, or nearly so. I'd never been keen on revising, even in school where it was preached. Revising was fine for other, less talented writers, I thought; I preferred to write, save, and start something new. I'd even lost the habit of reading what I'd written once finished, because I couldn't take the inevitable dismay upon learning how my beautiful words and scenes and images and characters and insights had been disfigured in my absence, transformed into awkward, clanging, imprecise phrases, clichés, pretention, sentimentality, stereotypes, and basic confusion. So I printed the requisite pages, shoved them into envelopes, and sent them off to be judged by important people in big universities—who surely knew talent when they saw it. Before I knew it, the deadlines of the other programs had passed, so I shrugged them off and left it at that, two opposing futures: North, South; Rebel, Yank. I was ready to be anyone, as long as it wasn't me.

Chapter Thirteen

Cloudbreak

A number of developments complicated my life by the time Dad dropped by my apartment that summer. First, Gaby showed up, unannounced and illegal, having hitched to Tijuana, where she'd crossed the border in the company of a Mexican American family she'd befriended. We moved from Three Arch into a cheap apartment in Dana Point, and I helped get her a job in housekeeping at the Ritz.

The graduate program in New York turned me down, but the one in Atlanta extended me an offer. By this time, however, I wasn't so sure I wanted more school, and so I hadn't yet responded. Certainly, I couldn't see bringing Gaby all the way to Atlanta. Already, we lived two separate lives, mine in English, hers in Spanish, and both of us had given up trying to meld the two together. Through friends she met at the Ritz, she'd immersed herself in the local Mexican community, where no English was necessary. We didn't know each other's friends, and Gaby couldn't communicate with any of mine even if she wanted to. We met up at bedtime, and sometimes not even then.

Argentina still intrigued me, though bringing Gaby there was even less realistic than taking her to Atlanta. And finally, as I mulled my options, Brad from Human Resources suggested I apply for a fulltime job in his department. Apparently, I met the requirements: fluent Spanish and a college degree. I could do worse, he assured me. He himself had started as a server in the Terrace Café. And now he owned a house, had a wife, and was considering transferring to the Ritz on St. Thomas Island, where the staff wore open-necked linen instead of wool business suits. I had a week to think it over.

"I was driving by and thought you might want to hit The Cove," Dad said, and tossed me one of the two nectarines he'd brought. I'd ridden with him occasionally over the last months, but mainly I boarded with my friend from the Ritz, or paddled out solo. Surfers and spongers didn't generally hang together.

"Let me throw on some trunks," I said. I'd just gotten up and was wondering what to do with my day off. Gaby was out, either working or running around with her pot-smoking cohorts. I'd lost track of her schedule long ago. We'd become roommates who occasionally had sex. It seemed the thing we'd had before, the passion, had been a phenomenon of Mexico that no longer functioned in the U.S.

As usual, Dad and I had The Cove to ourselves. A residual El Niño swell hit a few days before, and surf was high up and down the coast. We paddled out, me on the sponge—now outfitted with an arm leash—and Dad on an old short board he'd traded for a bag of pot. We sat on our boards, watching the horizon, commenting on the lines coming in. That a set? No. Don't think so. Maybe it'll break over this way. Maybe. We caught some waves. Paddled back out. Caught some more. The water had warmed up enough that I wore only trunks and a wetsuit vest. The sun was bright in a cloudless sky. California!

We sat there, letting smallish waves go by for a while, waiting for a set. "You heard from Ole lately?" I asked. He'd gotten out of prison shortly after I'd moved out with Gaby. Gil and Helen allowed him to take my place in Casa Three Arch. He'd been doing surprisingly well. First, he found a job at the filling station outside the Three Arch gates, and he'd made friends with the local "grommets," the kids who hung around the beach at Three Arch. They thought he was cool, an authentic hood, the kind of guy you hear about but never meet in a place like Laguna. Plus, Ole had always been a sweet kid when not on drugs. He and I had even been developing something of a friendship, and I'd sometimes pick him up from work in the gigantic old Pontiac I'd bought for a thousand dollars, take him to my local dive bar, where his prison frame and scratchy tattoos didn't attract too much attention. I hoped during these times to show that it was possible to get high without ruining your life. You just have to follow a few basic rules. Drink as much alcohol as you like, but never use drugs. Never drive to the bar, and in fact, avoid driving as much as possible, even when sober. A lot of bad things can happen when you're behind the wheel. Finally, show up to work no matter how sick you feel. It'll teach you not to drink so much next time. But my wisdom was lost on Ole. He barely drank, for one thing.

"Looks like your brother's gone AWOL," Dad said. "Got a call from an old girlfriend in San Berdu. Next thing I know, he's gone. Missed work. Missed his parole meeting. Got a warrant out for his arrest now. He'll be back inside next time a cop decides to check him out."

"San Bernardino?" I asked, stomach churning with anger and disappointment. I'd actually begun to think Ole was finally done with that life, but he'd fooled me again. "Why would anyone leave Laguna for San Berdu? It's insane."

"The women out here aren't interested in a guy like Ole. They expect a certain, how shall we say, amount of money. He was probably horny, lonely. He also likes being high, likes that whole gangster life. Now and then I'd hear him on the phone with one of his old road dogs, and I got to say, he comes alive."

"Speaking of which," Dad said after a pause, "ran into Jeff the other day." He was talking about blond Jeff, his old surf partner. "He's been living outdoors, crashing on the beach. I think he's smoking crack."

"Crack? I didn't know you could get crack around here."

"Oh, yeah. You can get just about anything around here, or anywhere else for that matter. I tried to get him into the water, knock him back into his body, but he wouldn't do it. Too strung out."

"You think surfing's the answer to everything, don't you?"

"Maybe. I think Americans have lost touch with their bodies. They've got all this money, but they're so fat they can hardly walk. The way I see it, your body's the vehicle that carries around your brain, your soul if you like. These people are too lazy to bring it in for an oil change, much less a tune up."

Dad had completed parole without a hitch. His vices, coffee and pot, were harmless. He was mellowing out these days, less angry, less inclined to complain about everything. Getting older, I supposed. I hadn't heard about his surf ranch in Baja lately, and I assumed that hadn't worked out. He'd obviously dropped his earlier plan to relocate to the Philippines once off parole, especially after learning that his common-law wife there had found a new man. No further word about reconnecting with his old prison pals either. He'd done three years of a six-year sentence for involuntary manslaughter, a light sentence, to be sure, but not an unfair one, I decided. He wasn't going to hurt anyone, not again.

"You've gotten pretty good on that thing," he said, pointing with his chin at my board.

"I guess I've figured it out a little. Aliso teaches you fast."

"Sometimes I'll pull over on the road and watch that wave. It's definitely an adrenaline trip. You'd have been a big wave rider, I reckon, if you'd gotten into it earlier."

I breathed in deeply and let it out. If only, I thought, imagining a different life, a life as a regular kid at the beach, happy, spoiled, proud to have never lived anywhere but Laguna, Corona, Newport, or wherever I'd have grown up, a surfer kid. Probably I've have been good at that kind of life. A pair of dolphins happened by just then, traveling south fifteen feet out from us. "Look at that," I said.

"Uh, huh. Flipper."

"Should we check them out?" I asked, and slid to my belly to paddle. Dolphins weren't rare, but I'd never before seen them quite this close by.

"Naw. Let them do their thing. We'll do ours. Everybody's happier that way."

I sat up and watched them pass, a pair, and then two more, and two more after those, smooth heads followed by the arching back and a fin. "Sometimes they'll catch a wave with you," Dad said. "Sea lions like to surf too. Pretty sure they do it for the same reason we do. Here we go," he said, and pointed to a white explosion of foam a good hundred feet outside. "Cloudbreak," Dad said, and began to paddle out. I didn't know what that meant, but I didn't have time to think about it. I kicked hard after Dad, toward a great, rising wall of water. He took off to the right while I shot up and over. I caught the next one, this one a left, about twelve feet high. As I slid along the top of the face, waiting to plunge down, I realized I was heading the wrong direction, toward the break, so I jerked the board 180 degrees to the right, sped down to the bottom, gathering enough speed to shoot back up, and then down again. Halfway to shore the wave lost power, but then gathered itself again, broke from top to bottom. I stalled by dragging my right hand through the face, ducked into the curl for a few seconds, and then rode the diminishing wave all the way to the sand.

Calm returned after the set, and I paddled through milky, aerated water. The dolphins had passed. "That was fun," I said, joining Dad outside.

"You got the best wave so far. Real nice how you tucked into that little curl at the end. One of the benefits of a Boogie, I guess. Everything's overhead." He was sitting up, absently splashing water onto his shoulders. "Gil said something about you applying for a suit job at the hotel."

"I haven't yet, but I'm thinking about it."

I told him about the job, and then school, and Argentina. "And then there's Gaby," I concluded, and shared some of my misgivings on that front.

"Gaby's a very pretty girl," Dad said. "As for the other stuff..." he chuckled. "You know me. I always follow the path of least resistance. You remind me of Susan."

"I've heard that," I said.

"She was one of those fish that want to live in the middle of the biggest reef around, right there in the food chain where it's all happening. You're like that too."

I hopped to my knees on the board and allowed myself to tip over into the water, just to get wet. "Maybe so," I said, arms draped over the board. "I'm not going to apply for the Ritz job," I said, having made a decision just then. "I'm not sure what I'll do, but at least I can rule that one out."

"I can see why," he said. "I guess you'll be leaving one way or another. Wish you weren't though." He lifted palms full of water and watched it drain through his fingers. "You're good to surf with, you know?"

"Yeah," I said, climbing back onto my board. "You too." And then we sat silent, a little embarrassed, facing the horizon, waiting for the next wave to come and carry us to shore.

Chapter Fourteen

Argentina

I came upon a man drinking Modelo beer from a can in the neighborhood where Elizabeth Taylor and Richard Burton carried on back when Vallarta was in the news. The beer drinker stood on a stone wall that held back the hillside, speaking fluent Spanish to three locals in tee shirts who sat along the wall at his feet. Green jeweled cufflinks flashed as he tipped the can.

"Hey, friend," he assailed me in an American accent. "Care for a beer?"

I looked around to be sure he was talking to me. "Why not?" I answered, and one of his cohorts produced a can from a paper bag.

"What's your story?" the man in cufflinks asked, hopping down from the wall.

"Mine?" I paused to pop the beer. "Not much of a story. House sitting right now, but that ends soon. Hoping to catch a flight to Buenos Aires once the prices drop."

Two weeks before, my Vallarta friend Mark—the Aussie I'd shared slimy mushrooms with—sent me an email, explaining how he'd scored a gig house-sitting for the rainy season. The place was amazing: swimming pool, maid, three stories, satellite television, internet, ocean view. How about I come down and spell him a week? He loved the house but was itching to get out of town for a while. This was the sign I'd been waiting for, so I sprang into action. First I donated the Pontiac to my mom and

Ralph, and they drove Gaby and I to Mexicali, where we took a bus to Guadalajara. I stayed with her and her family for a couple of days, and then she went with me to the familiar bus station that served Vallarta. As the passengers boarded, I kissed her goodbye for the final time. She hugged me tight and didn't say a word, not even goodbye. She smiled and waved as the bus pulled away, and for a moment I thought I'd made a big mistake letting her go. But then she was out of sight, and I settled into my decision.

I'd returned to Vallarta for two reasons: to bring Gaby home, and because I figured flights from Mexico City or Guadalajara would be cheaper than those from Los Angeles. But so far, several hours of searching online had revealed prices every bit as high as those in California. Just a quirk, I told myself, and set about to wait them out. Surely they'd drop.

"Where are you going to stay when the owners come back?" the cufflink man asked.

"Not sure," I said. "If I could find some work, I might be interested in renting an apartment."

"Work," he said, flicking the idea away with a long-fingered hand. "My name's Arthur, Arturo, whatever you like. I can find you a job in a second, if that's what you're after, but first I've got to show you this apartment that'd be perfect for you. It's beautiful, man, and a crazy-good deal. This guy I know owns it. He doesn't care about money. Just wants the place occupied. Once you get set up, then we'll talk about a job. I know everyone around here. I've lived in Vallarta my whole life. Come on."

He tossed the can into a bin while his friends watched silently. I couldn't read their attitudes. Arturo walked up the path a few steps and stood waiting. "Well? You coming?"

It was daytime and the streets were crowded. I was curious, so I followed him, up a cobbled road that narrowed into a maze of footpaths, twisting left and right and always climbing. "The owner," Arturo explained, dripping sweat but not slowing down, "wants someone who'll take care of the place. Are you responsible?"

"Yes," I said.

"Clean?"

"That too."

"Okay, we'll see."

Ten minutes later, the path leveled out, and we climbed a steep set of stairs that led back toward the coast. Arturo unlocked the door at the top, and we entered a room that opened to a large deck. Once through the sliding glass doors, I grew dizzy. The ocean looked different from up here, paler and softer, as if viewed from a jet. To the left and right was open air and rooftops below. We surely stood at the highest point in Vallarta. "How much?" I asked, imagining waking to this view the rest of my days.

"Three hundred U.S. a month," Arturo said, fiddling with a link.

"Sorry," I said. "Out of my league."

"No problem. Like I said, money's not the issue. I can tell my friend would like you. How about two hundred?"

"Two hundred? Wow. Sounds like a deal. I might think about it next week when the house sitting ends. What about that job you mentioned?"

"The job is easy, but this'll be gone by next week. One fifty. That's as low as I can go. Otherwise my friend will kill me."

I looked down on the ocean, at a dozen small white triangles, sailboats heading out to sea or coming home. "I don't see how anyone could rent this place for one fifty," I said.

"You'd be surprised," Arturo replied in a new, cold voice. "Nobody can fill these places. The rental market sucks."

I stepped away from the rail, alarmed by Arturo's lie. Earlier that day, Mark had assured me that foreigners were moving to Vallarta from all over, grabbing up everything; the rent for my own former apartment had doubled since I'd gone. "Take them," Arturo said, jingling the keys. He grabbed my wrist and slapped the keys into my palm. I pulled free and the keys hit the deck planks. "Just a little deposit," Arturo said, stooping. "500 pesos to hold it. If not, I can't promise anything."

"I'll think about it," I said. "If you rent it out, good for you. If not, maybe I'll be back."

Arturo lifted his wide, bony shoulders. His face had seemed handsome a few minutes ago but now looked skeletal, the cheekbones prominent and the eye sockets filled with shadow. I left the apartment and walked back to Mark's.

"There you are," he said. He sat at the kitchen table with photography proofs spread before him. He'd been working on a career as a travel photographer, and had so far sold some photos to an adventure clothing company. He was hoping to pick up some momentum with this latest trip. "Where've you been?"

I told him about the apartment and Arturo.

"One fifty?" he asked. "That is an amazing price. I wouldn't mind having a look myself."

Just before dusk that evening, I took Mark up the hill to see the apartment, figuring he'd at least be able to record the address for later, even if we didn't manage to get inside. As luck would have it, Arturo was there, sitting on the bottom of the stairway, hugging his knees to his chest and rocking a little. "Arturo," I said, "this is my friend Mark."

"I'm sorry," Arturo whined, cringing as if expecting to be hit. "I don't have anything."

"I don't know what you're sorry about," I informed him. "We're here to see the apartment, if it's still available."

"The apartment?" he asked, uncurling like a pill bug. "Just a minute. I need cigarettes."

Mark offered him a Marlboro, and Arturo looked at the pack as if he'd never seen anything like it. He began to walk away from the apartment.

We followed. "As I said before," I called, jogging up to Arturo, "I can't afford the place right now, but Mark might be interested."

"Wait!" Arturo said, and ducked behind us. "Do you see anyone in that car?" he whispered.

"What car?" Jalopies were parked end to end all along the summit summit road.

"That one!" He pointed to a VW Bug, totally empty as far as I could tell, just like the car parked behind it and the one before it.

"No," I said.

"Are you sure there's not four people in it? Maybe two? A man with curly hair and a woman?"

"I'm pretty sure. I'm looking right at it and there's no one in that car, unless they're lying down on the seats."

"Okay. Let's go." And he led us down a path to a tiny general store.

"What do you smoke?" I asked.

"Smoke?" Arturo said, and plucked a canister from a rack. "*Bolsa, por favor*," he said to the cashier, who placed the can in a plastic bag.

"Arturo," I said on the way back, interrupting some internal monologue he seemed to be engaged in. "You there? My friend here is interested in seeing the apartment. Are you with me?"

"I'm an addict," Arturo confessed, shaking his head slowly as we approached the stairs. "No better than a junky," he added, laughing bitterly as he ascended two steps at a time.

"You're right about the view," Mark said. Arturo was squatting at the end of the deck. "I'd have paid three hundred easy for this place. More than a bargain. Too good to be true, really."

"Want some?" Arturo asked, kneeling with the plastic bag held open on the deck before him. Without waiting for an answer, he sprayed whatever was in the canister into the bag, brought the bag to his face and began to pant.

"No thanks," I said.

Flat on his back in the center of the deck, Arturo rolled his head side to side. "I wasn't always like this," he murmured. "My dad owns half of Vallarta. Mom makes pottery in Santa Barbara. I know people. I used to sell houses. Then I closed timeshare. I was a closer," he shouted, "not one of the clowns that wear you down all day. That's big money, closing. Not just anyone can do it. It takes something special. But I haven't made a sale in...shit. I don't know. Now they don't even want me coming around the hotels. How's that for loyalty?"

"This place isn't yours to rent, is it?" I asked.

He only laughed. He'd apparently been squatting here, some apartment overlooked by a rental agency, collecting phony deposits every chance he got. Suddenly, I felt unsafe. How many enemies had Arturo made over the last weeks, enemies that knew his address? Would these furious victims discriminate between the guilty and innocent, between Arturo and me? How far down to the rooftops below? "Let's split," I said to Mark, and we left Arturo to the mess he'd made of his life.

"Nice place," Mark said, and that was the last word on it.

Mark took off the next day, leaving me master of a house a couple of blocks from where Liz and Richard had lived famously in sin. I watched a lot of television over the next few days, while checking airline prices compulsively. At first, the prices stayed level, and then they began to rise. I lived on the dregs of the refrigerator but still managed to spend money. As things stood, the ticket alone would about clean me out. If I acted now, I'd arrive nearly broke. Perhaps, if I got a job immediately, I could pull it off. With this in mind, I navigated to an ESL website, but I didn't find jobs advertised. Instead, I read post after post complaining of high unemployment in Buenos Aires, of stiff competition among English teachers, of low wages and expensive housing. Whiners, I decided, complainers. Only losers bothered to post their stories like this. The others were too busy working. That's what I told myself, but I didn't believe it. Obviously, I wasn't the first gringo to have dreamed of escaping to Argentina, and, unlike so many others, I didn't even have a teaching certificate.

The rain came down hard the morning before Mark was to return, hiding the ocean and knocking out the satellite television. All day I roamed the house, opening cabinets. The owners apparently read nothing but *Condé Nast* and had emptied the place of liquor. I started writing a story about a taco vendor, but he didn't do anything aside from vend tacos. My attempts to liven his day failed: hacking an impertinent gringo with his cleaver, falling for a beautiful but cruel tourist, inventing a sauce so hot it killed everyone who tried it. The stories kept ending too quickly or not at all. I should have taken the job at the Ritz, I thought, toasting a stale tortilla on a burner. I should have earned an ESL certificate like Brett. I should have stayed in San Francisco. I should have married my first true love and adopted her son way back when I first graduated high school. Anything but what I'd done. I lay curled on the couch, watching a million raindrops pit the swimming pool. At three in the afternoon, the rain let up, so I thought to hell with it, filled my pocket with pesos and hustled out to a little bar I'd often passed down the lane.

The inside of La Revolución looked like a shaded version of the world outside. A mossy old fountain bubbled in the center of the cobblestone floor, and the green, corrugated fiberglass roof filled the place in weird light and the patter of rain. A small mango tree grew in the corner, among lesser forms of vegetation. It was the best bar ever. I sat on a stool and ordered beer over ice with lime and salt. Though rainy, it was hot as ever. A few patrons, white-collar Mexicans by their looks, sat at tables, and I shared the bar with a weary-looking gringo with limp, pale hair. *¿Hablas ingles?* he croaked, with no attempt at a Mexican accent. He appeared sickly in the greenish light, and his eyes were so watery I thought he might have been crying.

"Yes, I speak English," I said.

"I see you're drinking."

"I am. So are you."

"Yes." He lifted an empty Pacifico bottle beside his glass of melted ice. "*Otro*," he said to the bartender, a woman with the round face and narrow eyes of a Mayan.

"I believe the word is *otra*," I said.

"Forgive me."

We spoke across the space between us, my first conversation since Mark had left. When I returned from the bathroom I took the stool next to him. His name was Lane, and his red-rimmed eyes drooped like a bloodhound's. His accent was New England, and he seemed a man of breeding, around fifty years old, not at the top of his game. He'd been living in Vallarta for several years. I gathered his income was fixed and that he drank daily.

We spoke of Mexico, travel in general, Vallarta, the expatriate community of Yelapa south of Vallarta, accessible only by boat. We spoke of drinking: tequila, whiskey, martinis, beer, and the micheladas— beer, ice, and lime—we were currently downing one after the other. I began to share my worries about the future. The Argentina plan wasn't looking good. I'd already thrown away the hotel gig. Graduate school? It seemed a waste of time, aside from the fact that I'd ignored the invitation. What the hell was I doing with my life?

"Don't bother trying to earn money," Lane advised.

"How's that?"

"You can work until you drop dead and never win that game. It's fixed. If you weren't born with money, there's only one other way to get it. Marriage. Start developing your charm. I'd say you've got about five years of looks left. Use them wisely."

"Is that what you did?" I asked, and Lane only laughed.

I looked up from my empty glass and found that the scene had changed. A man was now tending bar, in place of the Mayan. He didn't seem friendly, the rain had stopped, and it was dark outside. "Time to move on," Lane said. "Care to join me?" He gathered himself and walked out with the help of a cane. "Broke my leg a few years ago," he said as we exited. "Never healed right."

"How'd you break it?"

"Don't remember," he admitted. "Maybe I fell. Maybe a car ran over me."

We resumed the drinking in one of the big bars across from the boardwalk where I'd met Gaby. The prices were high, but I didn't care anymore. The bar soon became too noisy for talk, so we set off again. "What about here?" I asked, gesturing toward a gringo-style bar and grill.

"I'm afraid I'm no longer welcome in that establishment," Lane said.

"You're banned from a bar, in Mexico?"

"Indeed I am. Stabbed my friend with a steak knife. Even Mexicans tend to frown on that kind of behavior."

"What were you doing with a steak knife?" I asked.

"Eating *carne asada*. Or so I assume. I don't remember that particular evening. I certainly woke with a hangover though, in jail no less. Cost me a lot of money to get out of that jam." Lane sighed. "That was three years ago, and Richie, my friend, still won't talk to me. I've got it," he said, and waved his cane at the street. In moments, a taxi pulled over.

"Where to?" I asked, sliding into the back seat.

"You'll like it," he assured me.

We drove out of town, under the inland highway and up a winding road into the hills. Soon we pulled into a large, dirt parking lot outside a low-flung building. A blue neon sign on the roof read La Luna Llena, and muffled dance music emanated from inside. Lane paid our covers, and we were shown to a small table near a stage. The place was clean, air conditioned, and flashing under strobe and spot lights. White cloths draped the tables, attended by servers in crisp uniforms. A beautiful young woman strutted across the stage, naked except for high heeled shoes.

We ordered Pacificos. The dancer stood still for a moment, ignoring the music and treating everyone to a pissed-off, haughty expression, as if the men throwing bills onto the stage weren't worthy to lick her spiked heels, and she was right about that. A knock-out, cut from the pages of a magazine, leggy, thin, and flawless under the stage lights, she traipsed across the stage like a fashion model, as if draped in silk and fur. I appreciated the fearlessness, but she scared and depressed me. I set one of Lane's bills onto the stage and looked away when she met my eyes.

The song ended and she picked up her panties and cash, the only ungraceful move of her act. She exited through the left side of the stage as another girl emerged from the right. The new stripper wore a yellow bikini and laughed as she danced a silly, self-mocking dance. She struggled, or pretended to struggle, to unclip her top, and then she swirled it burlesque style and flung it back against the curtain. So different, this one from the last, I thought, staring at the faintest appendectomy scar on her belly. Whereas the previous girl's face was a hard triangle, this one's was oval, nose a bit wide. She smiled often, showing slightly crooked front teeth. These perceived imperfections, these signals of indigenous blood, had forced her into the comedy routine, I deduced, even though she was beautiful by any definition. I got angry. She was worth ten of that first beauty. I grabbed two bills and stood. She danced toward me, moving her fists up and down as if milking a cow, until she came to the edge of the stage and paused, hands on her hips, her belly button even with my face. It was flat, neither inny nor outy, and I longed to kiss it. I looked up and she slowly crouched. I smelled her breath, clean and sweet, like a child's. I tried to hand the bills to her, but she shook her head, no, then pointed south and rose, jutting a hip. I tucked the bills under the bikini string, and she kissed her hand and placed it on my forehead.

An intense feeling of love signaled that I was very drunk, but I didn't care. My drunkenness was part of the whole perfection of the moment.

"I think I'll switch to vodka tonic," Lane said, and I realized I'd forgotten to drink my beer. I chugged at it, so as not to fall behind. My dancer left and another replaced her. Over the next hour, a parade of beauties took the stage, but I didn't have the energy to distinguish them. Then the haughty one returned, and I calculated that, if the loop held, my girl was next. *You don't have to do this*, I imagined saying, or just mouthing. But when she came around I placed another bill in her bikini and looked at her sadly, hoping to communicate disapproval of the men who had used the bill placing as an excuse to grope and to pull her panties aside to get a closer view than was otherwise warranted. I'd been watching them all night, fatsos in ties; I hated their sausage fingers and black mustaches, and I burned with possessiveness when they pawed my girl. How she must despise them, I thought, and the lights came on. "What do you think of her?" I asked Lane.

"Who?"

"The funny girl."

"Funny? I'm not sure about funny. They're all pretty though. And young." He brought the glass to his mouth. "I must tell you, it's a relief not to care anymore. You can't believe it right now, but one of these days you're going to look at girls like this, and they won't mean anything. And you know what? You'll be thankful. This next part's interesting."

The haughty girl threw aside a black curtain and strode out in a miniskirt and tube top. The rest of the dancers followed. They began to make the rounds, collecting extra tips, greeting the fans, and so on. Mine emerged in the middle of the pack, and I began to compose a speech. Soon the speech was a dialog. *Come home with me, and I'll make you the most delicious breakfast you've ever tasted.*

No one's ever offered me breakfast before.

Of course not! These cretins? Have you ever dreamed of traveling around the world? Did I mention I'm staying in a mansion?

As I rehearsed, the first dancer disappeared through the curtain with one of the fat businessmen. I wondered how much she charged, and for what, and I wondered if she held her poise throughout the act. Musing, I lost track of my girl until she pulled a chair up to our table and sat beside me. "Hola, güero," she said. All gringos were *güeros* in Vallarta. It meant something like blondie, or maybe whitey. It didn't seem to matter that my hair was dark.

"Hola," I said, and out it all came, a gush of Spanish: What are you doing here? You're too good for this place. Let's go home together. I'll show you a new life. We'll travel. We'll live in a hut on a beach. I'll catch fresh fish for dinner.

I was so caught up in my speech, I didn't notice the effect it was having until her face had blossomed fully with derision. "I think you're really funny," I concluded.

"All the men who come here think I'm funny," she replied. "Three hundred pesos." And she pointed toward the curtain, from which her rival emerged as if victorious. A moment later, her customer stepped out timidly, slinked up the side of the room and out.

"I'm sorry," I said, and couldn't think of the Spanish words for the rest. I gave her the last of Lane's bills. She smiled, leaned forward, kissed my forehead and moved on to the next table. "I'm ready to go," I told Lane.

"Meet you outside," he said. "I've got to use the restroom."

By the hostess station, I couldn't resist glancing back in time to see my dancer, who obviously wasn't mine, walking toward the curtain, customer in tow.

I stepped out the front door, into a cluster of cabbies. "One moment," I told them, shaking off the sting of unrequited love. "I'm waiting for my friend."

I stood for a while, listening to the cabbies mutter among themselves, and Spanish once again began to percolate in me. I rallied against self pity, replacing it with arrogance. Here I was, in this foreign country, able to speak a language nobody I knew at home could talk. "How are you tonight, señores?" I asked, voice like a timeshare salesman's.

They nodded their heads grimly.

"Why so unhappy, with so many beautiful women around?"

"You like our women?" one of them asked.

I looked over the bunch, all shorter than I was. I didn't know which one of them had spoken. "Of course!" I said. "Who doesn't love women, especially Mexican women! The most beautiful in the world. But I won't pay." I shrugged. "I want them to want me, not my money," I concluded, and one of the cabbies stepped up to me. I couldn't see his face in the dark, but his head was large like Francisco's, my old Ritz companion.

"What are you doing in Vallarta?" he asked. I just about slapped him companionably on the shoulder, but something in his tone gave me pause.

"Oh, this and that," I said. "House sitting for some rich gringos. Teaching English. Whatever I can find. Why do you ask? You know where a guy like me can make some money?"

The little guy reached into his pocket and withdrew his wallet. He opened it, revealing an identification card and a badge. "I am Bartolo Villahermosa, the Chief of Police of Puerto Vallarta. Show me your papers."

While short, Villahermosa wasn't as little as I'd thought. He outweighed me by fifty pounds. His shoulders were wide like a bull's, and, I saw as he shifted into the neon light of the club's sign, his nose was smashed flat across his square face. A black pistol rested in a holster at his hip. I plunged my hands into my pockets, looking for something that might save me.

"I'm sorry," I said in Spanish, and came out with a twenty peso bill and some coins, an entirely insufficient bribe. I'd left my passport at home.

"No papers?" he asked, shaking his head as if the situation were very grave, very grave indeed, which it was. "Working in Mexico without a permit? Traveling without a passport?"

"Oh, no, not working. I was just kidding, just bragging. We can get my passport. It's in town. I'll take you there."

He shook his head slowly. "We will go to the station," he announced, his first words in English.

I swooned a bit, but otherwise felt all-too sober, the coins and bill resting uselessly in my hand. The cabbies were all looking away, embarrassed. Villahermosa was showing off for them, just as I'd been showing off a moment before.

"Please," I said, desperately trying to think of some remedy, and then the door opened behind me.

"Lane!" cried the chief, flinging his arms wide. "My good friend Lane! So nice to see you! What are you doing here? Looking at the *muchachas?*" He wagged a finger in Lane's face, squinting humorously. "That's very bad."

Lane looked at me. At the chief. At the cabbies who were pointedly not looking at anyone. "Just having some drinks with this young man," he said, and I could have kissed him.

"This kid?"

"Yeah."

"You're with this kid?" The chief's incredulity was gigantic.

"Sure."

The chief was shaking his head, stunned. "This kid's no good," he finally declared.

"Oh, he's not bad."

"I don't like him. He's lying to me."

I thought about jumping in to defend myself, but kept my mouth shut.

"I don't know anything about that," Lane said.

"Tell me, what is this kid doing here in my country?"

"Oh…" Lane lifted his hands noncommittally, and the chief grinned, having caught the gringos once again. "House sitting," Lane remembered at the last second. "Spending some dollars. You know."

The chief frowned deeply at me. He paused for a long time, shaking his head, puzzling it out. Then he smiled and patted me, harder than necessary, on the top of the head. "Okay. Lane like you." Now he was painfully massaging my neck. "I like you." He turned to Lane. "You like the girls? I know this one like the girls! You need a ride? Come with me."

We got into the back of his car, an unmarked sedan, and it occurred to me that we might be prisoners after all. The chief pulled out of the parking lot and drove toward town like a stock car racer, fast and skillfully, squealing around sharp turns within inches of long drops down the mountain. I was too stunned to be scared.

He took us into town and parked in front of a cartoonish mural of an evil wolf painted over an entire wall, the door included. I'd passed this mural dozens of times when I'd lived in town, and had always taken it for an abandoned shop of some sort. The chief let us out, and he knocked on the door. A secret knock, I realized. The door opened, and we entered a smoky room, crowded with men. "I leave you here," the chief said. "Enjoy. Lane, you come by my house sometime. My wife asks about you. Okay? And you," he said to me, "watch out." He joined two other men and disappeared through an interior door.

The wolf bar was small, close, and smoky. A dancer swayed listlessly on a raised stage, under a ceiling so low she had to duck her head. Her hair was frizzy and her body paunchy. Nobody, including her, had any interest in her dance. We ordered beer. I tried to pay the boy who'd popped the cans, but he waved his hands and backed away.

We sat at a small table near the front door, choking down warm Modelo like children eating their broccoli. I made sure the chief wasn't in sight and leaned forward until my head almost touched Lane's. "Who was that?" I whispered.

"That," Lane said, "is one serious asshole."

"Is he really the Chief of Police?"

Lane nodded. "Chief gangster too. They say he and his brother once got caught with a trunk full of cocaine they'd just confiscated. The men who had them took back the drugs and made Bartolo and his brother stand beside the road. They shot the brother in the head and Bartolo in both knees. He's been taking it out on the rest of us ever since."

"Jesus," I said. We guzzled the dregs of the beer and left the wolf bar.

Lane hailed a cab and offered me a ride home. On the way, we stopped at a liquor store, where Lane hobbled up to the outdoor counter and returned with a large cardboard box. He placed the box between us on the seat, a case of beer and three jumbo bottles of liquor. I figured we were about to go to some enormous party Lane had in store for us, another surprise that lifted my mood. But then Lane asked me where I lived.

"Calle Ecuador," I told the cabbie.

We drove along the rough cobbled streets, the bottles clinking. "What's with the booze?" I asked.

"Oh," Lane said, shifting on the seat to settle in. "I'm a bad alcoholic. I get very sick if I wake up without anything to drink in the morning. It's not pretty."

I didn't have anything to say to that, and when the taxi stopped before the big house, I felt so lonely it hurt. I wanted to invite Lane in for a nightcap, but I could see by the cab's clock that it was five in the morning, and Lane had already hired a taxi and bought his liquor and was ready for home. The night couldn't go on forever. I paused at the door, searching for something to say.

"Yes?" Lane asked.

"I'll catch you later," I said, though I knew I'd never see him again.

Inside, I turned on the computer and waited for the dial up to connect. I was so drunk I could barely type, but eventually I managed to confirm that the cost of flights to Argentina had not dropped. Waiting for a competing travel site to load, I rested my head on the desk and woke an instant later to sounds like warfare. I nearly dropped to the floor and hid under the desk, but then realized the noise was merely the maid running the vacuum downstairs. It was tomorrow, now today, another gray morning, and I was still quite drunk. I turned off the computer and stumbled into the bathroom to drink water from the tap. My eyes were small, red, and mean looking. The right side of my face bore a red blotch where it had rested on the computer keyboard. Aching in the head and joints and guts, I recalled vividly every stupid utterance and thought from the night before, inanity after inanity, shame upon shame. Not just last night. My whole life. The memories flashed like cards through my mind. What a loser I was. Lower than low. That love nonsense to the stripper! The boasts to the cabbies! What a fool, what a drunk. Was I really going to Argentina to make something of myself? Not a chance. I'd be back in California in a waiter costume in three months. I was no adventurer, no artistic, romantic soul adrift in the world. I wasn't interesting. What was I? A thirty-year-old unemployed food server. A cheap American. An ugly American. A low-budget vacationer. A lush.

I escaped the riotous vacuuming. Hunched as if gut shot, I shuffled down the hill, hopelessly trying to escape my own boozy stink. I passed under the footbridge that had linked the rooftops of Richard Burton and Elizabeth Taylor's temporary mansions. They'd been married to others during filming of the movie that had put Vallarta on the map, and the local Catholics hadn't appreciated the flaunted adultery. Nuns began to show up outside the movie set to protest, in easy view of a dozen gossip reporters' cameras. So Burton had paid a visit to the monsignor. "Listen, chum, about these protests."

"Yes?"

"That dome of yours, what happened?"

"Unfortunately, señor, it was God's will that an earthquake destroy it."

"I see. How much would it take to replace a dome like that?"

"Oh, ten thousand of your American dollars, I should think."

Burton wrote a check. The nuns remembered "thou shall not judge." The church got a new dome. The movie was a big hit. God's will be done. Redemption, I thought, staggering into a shop that supplied international phone and internet service, wasn't cheap.

The boy at the desk showed me to a booth. I followed the instructions and dialed the number scrawled on a piece of paper in my wallet. "English Department," said the woman on the other end.

"Yes. Hi. I was accepted into your Master's of Fine Arts program a few months back."

"Uh huh?"

"Can I still go?"

"Well. I'm not sure. Classes start in four days."

"If I show up, will you let me stay?" I could hear breathing on the other end, the sound of someone across the world in Atlanta, Georgia. "I'm calling from Mexico," I added, for no real reason.

"What's your name? Hold please."

The moments were dollars, a stack of them whirring like shuffled cards. But what could I do but wait?

"Okay," she said. "I just talked to the director of graduate studies. Why didn't you contact us when we sent the offer?"

"Good question. I've been trying to figure a few things out. I'm really sorry I didn't do what I was supposed to do."

"Well, Dr. McHaney said you can still enroll. Only we can't offer you an assistantship."

"That means no money? How will I survive?"

"The English Department can't offer you one this semester, but if you look around, you might find something."

"But I'm broke."

"Like I said. We can't offer an assistantship this semester. Spring maybe."

"You said there are other options."

"Some students find assistantships in other departments. It's a large campus. Also, you'd better fill out a FAFSA form right away if you want a loan."

"So you're saying it's likely I'll find some kind of funding."

"In the past, other students have found assistantships outside the English Department."

"Great. So there's funding available. I'll see you Monday."

I hung up before she could repeat that other students had found assistantships in the past. I packed and caught the first bus heading north. The picture in my mind of Buenos Aires faded with every mile, a photograph left out in the sun too long. The sidewalk café disappeared first, and then, one by one, the beautiful women walking by, until only I remained, floating in a formless gray fog that finally swallowed me up.

Chapter Fifteen

Atlanta

On a redeye flight somewhere over the center of the country, my ankles began to itch. I tried to ignore the maddening burn and tickle, but eventually I gave in to a furious bout of two-handed scratching until both ankles bled. In Hartsfield International, I caught an elevated train, from which I watched the city approach. It was eight in the morning, and already a hard white sun was up, revealing an expanse of brick buildings consumed by vines, a tangle of freeways, and a nest of glimmering skyscrapers. The feeling was of decay and shiny new growth.

The train roared into a tunnel. Deep under the city, I lugged my bags through the central metro station and boarded another train. A half hour later, I arrived in Decatur, where I'd booked a bed at a youth hostel. I hauled the bags into an elevator that smelled so strongly of piss my eyes watered. Up top, I stepped out into thick damp heat.

I found no cabs waiting at the station. My bags were so heavy I could only drag them a few intense steps at a time before resting. None of the loiterers outside the dodgy Chinese take-out joint offered to help, and I didn't ask. An hour later, soaked like a marathon runner, I completed the five blocks to the hostel. In the shower, I couldn't help raking my fingernails over the rash that had now crept up to my thighs.

The next day, M onday, red, oozing bumps covered my body.

Scratching wildly, I walked around the university, more a collection of office buildings than a proper campus, pleading with department secretaries who'd send me to yet other department secretaries. Finally, I found my way into the English as a Second Language Lab, where a woman offered me an assistantship on the spot, owing to my teaching experience at The USA School.

That afternoon, I attended a class on teaching composition to first-year college students. Afterward, I visited the tiny health center, where the lone nurse conjectured I was having an allergic reaction to some poison ivy-like plant I'd contacted in Mexico. Apparently, I'd been spreading the rash over my body by scratching. I was given a cream that smelled like Limburger cheese and seemed to have no effect on my skin. After dinner at the Chinese restaurant, I settled into the hostel common area to write my first paper, typing on an outdated laptop while young backpackers partied around me. The paper, a five pager, was my initial shot at a theory of teaching freshmen to write college papers, which was a good thing for me to think about because—the professor assured us—we'd be doing a lot of it in the future.

I received a "check plus," though I got the feeling the professor hadn't actually read the paper. The rash cleared up over the next couple of weeks. The trick was not to scratch, no matter how badly I wanted to.

◆

Friday found me haunting Periodicals, again. This was October, well into my first semester. Ambling along the "current issues" racks, I came upon a magazine called *Corrections Today*. I couldn't help leafing through its glossy pages, darkly fascinated by ads for waterproof mattresses, plastic shavers that can't be made into weapons, and reviews of the latest nonlethal incapacitation devises. Ole was back inside. I didn't bother to ask Mom what the charges were, or how long he'd been given. It wouldn't matter anyway. I came to the last page and replaced the magazine on the shelf. I considered scooping up the stack of past issues and taking them to my table for a thorough exploration, but I resisted this macabre urge and moved on.

I'd been scouring Periodicals since arriving in Atlanta, starting with photography and art magazines, moving through nature, politics, sports, literary journals, and finally anything with an interesting cover. I hadn't made any friends yet. Most of my classmates had gone directly from high school to undergraduate to grad school, all within the state of Georgia. They often still lived with their parents out in the suburbs. The older ones usually had families of their own, also in the suburbs. Even if they had lived nearby, I doubt we'd have hung around together. Anyone could see that we weren't from the same tribe.

I'd moved into a skuzzy apartment with a vegetarian feminist studying Community Psychology. She was a nice woman, smart and interesting, but again, we were from very different clans, and so we didn't bother socializing with one another. I spent my time studying, watching art films in the university cinema, taking long walks through the city, or hanging around the library. I didn't mind the loneliness. It somehow felt right.

Done with "current issues," I sat at a catalog computer and watched the cursor blink in the empty search field. For some reason, I couldn't think of a single author, or even a subject that presently interested me. I was as blank as the screen, until my fingers, on their own it seemed, typed "Cahuilla," the Indian tribe whose reservation had bordered our property in Anza. I hit the button, and one entry appeared: *Ethnography of the Cahuilla Indians*, published in 1908. It was located on the eighth floor, where I'd never had cause to visit, and so, vaguely curious, I entered the elevator. The door opened at my floor, and I was so surprised by what I saw I barely remembered to step off the elevator before the doors closed. She didn't seem real, the woman in the shiny red dress, bare leg bouncing over the other bare leg, lounging on a sofa that faced the elevator, as if she'd been waiting just for me. A very sexy black woman with straightened hair and muscular arms, she looked up from the book on her lap and smiled. I returned her smile and walked by, thinking that I should say or do something, but then it was too late. I was in the stacks.

By the time I found the book, a slight thing, I thought maybe I should go back and make some kind of bold move. Life affords certain opportunities, and so on. I pictured it like a headline. Lonely man meets lonely woman in the lonely stacks of a research library. It was like a movie, I thought, and then I thought some more. Like a movie, or a sting operation.

The woman in the red dress was a cop, I decided. A pervert had been lurking about this library over the last weeks, a specialist of the grope-and -run. He'd actually licked the bare ankle of one of my classmates. She'd been tripping her finger over titles when she felt a slimy sensation on the skin above her shoe. She'd screamed and jumped back as a head withdrew, turtle-like, into the gap in the bottom shelf. News of the pervert had eventually landed in the *Journal-Constitution*. In the article, the cops assured the public that they were on the case. That's why a pretty woman in a party dress had given me the green light on the forsaken eighth floor. She was trying to bait the creep. Solter had been right. There is no such thing as a free lunch.

Skimming the book, I learned that the Cahuilla subsisted mainly on acorns. They weaved baskets and burned their dead. They lived in huts built of mesquite, wore loin cloths, elected no leaders, and enforced no laws. They had public trials, of sorts, but no punishments. Those deemed guilty usually left on their own, out of shame. The ethnography was short, and focused mostly on the Cahuilla's material possessions, their migratory patterns, and their interactions with a dozen neighboring tribes. I wanted more, not just where they lived and what they did. I suddenly needed to know who they were.

I examined the book spines surrounding the ethnography, and eventually my hunt led me to a bibliography listing several consecutive issues of a certain anthropology journal, published throughout the 1920s.

At a nearby catalog, I found that the library held the journal, on this very floor, and soon I located them, green-bound books that took up a dozen feet of shelf space. I spread the relevant issues before me on the floor. They were all devoted to transcripts of interviews with Cahuilla tribesmen and women, people who had died long ago. I lay on my belly to read.

Most of these "informants" told some version of the Cahuilla origin story. It began with the twins, Mukat and Tamaioit, alone in the dark. They pulled tobacco, pipes, and tinder from their hearts. They lit up, and their sparks rose into the sky to become the stars; the smoke they blew swirled, turned solid, and that was the earth. This land needs people, Mukat told his brother. Who else will harvest the acorns? Tamaioit agreed, but that is where the agreement ended. The brothers were as different as two people could be. Mukat worked slowly, with great care and much thought, while Tamaioit threw his creatures together quickly, making snap decisions. When they had finished, Mukat scolded his brother for the sloppy work. Some of Tamaioit's creations had heads on both ends and others tails on both ends. Some too many legs, others no legs at all. These are no good, Mukat said. You must start over. But stubborn Tamaioit didn't want to start over. He was angry and ashamed, and so, after a long quarrel with his brother, he took his creatures below ground, causing the earth to shake so hard that everyone above fell to their sides and crawled about in terror. Finally the world settled, and Mukat was alone with the people he'd created, as well as a few of Tamaioit's that had stayed above, like Coyote and Duck and Taquitz.

I stared at the page. My Taquitz? Here in this book, written nearly a hundred years ago? I could picture the giant stone atop Taquitz Peak as clearly as I could see the pages before me; I could hear the precise timbre of my father's voice, telling me about Taquitz the child-killing chieftain. I hopped to my feet and walked up and down the aisles until I'd calmed enough to read on.

Mukat's creations became the First People, and for a time they prospered. Then Mukat's little sister arrived. Mılily was beautiful and wise. The people loved her, and she taught them their duties as men and women, husbands and wives, fathers and mothers. She showed them how to use the plants of the land, how to play games, celebrate, honor one another and the spirits of all things, how to build houses. All was well until Mukat came to desire her.

Mılily was offended. She left Mukat and the First People, rising into the sky, across which she traveled every night, revealing more and more of herself until she shined naked, nearly as bright as the sun; and then, just as slowly, she clothed herself in darkness until she disappeared, only to begin to undress once again. Mukat, angry and ashamed, created the rattlesnake and invented bows and arrows. At first, everyone agreed that the weapons helped them hunt, but then someone shot someone else, and the brother of the shot man shot the killer and became a killer himself. Soon, everyone had killed someone's brother, and everyone's brother had been killed. A wise woman gathered the people. Friends, she said, this can't go on. Mukat chased away our Mılily. He created the rattlesnake that bites and kills us. He gave us weapons, and we kill each other. It is all his fault. Instead of killing one another, we should kill him. That is how the First People decided to poison their creator.

The people offered Mukat water, and he drank deeply of it. As he languished, dying, only Coyote would visit. The rest were too ashamed of what they'd done. Mukat, Coyote said, look who's here. It's your only friend, Coyote. But Mukat knew Coyote and his tricks. To keep Coyote from stealing his power, he summoned the First People and asked them to burn his body immediately after he died. Sorry now for what they'd done, they placed his body on a large pile of sticks and lit it. But before the fire had finished its work, Coyote leaped into the flames and stole Mukat's heart. And that is how Coyote got some of Mukat's power but none of his wisdom.

After the death of Mukat, the First People became the spirits and animals of the earth, and their children were the Cahuilla. Some plants nourished, some plants healed, some plants killed, and others did nothing at all. They had to learn it all on their own. They found water underground, acorns in the trees and game in the bush. To honor Mukat, they burned their dead and mourned them at year's end. To honor Mílily, they married, raised children, and built shelters. They hunted with bow, arrow, and club. Life was hard, but they survived.

Satisfied with the origin story, I scanned the journals for mention of Taquitz. He appeared throughout. My father had been half right. Taquitz was known for kidnapping and killing children, and he had indeed been banished to the great mountain that now bears his name. But he wasn't a chieftain; he wasn't a flesh-and-blood man at all, at least according to the anthropologists. They called him a "culture hero," a trickster. He was both the morning star and the great stone peak into which it plunged. A shape-shifter, he appeared as a powerful warrior, an old white man who walked with a cane, or a slavering monster. He loved nothing more than taking children to his lair, where he'd eat them at his leisure.

One day, he captured a particularly willful young woman who just wouldn't stop talking. I miss my mother. I miss my father. I miss my friends. Let me go home. Day after day she kept at it, and for some reason, Taquitz couldn't seem to put an end to her prattle by simply eating her up. Finally, exasperated but somehow charmed, he agreed to set her free. On one condition. You must not, he told her, tell anyone what happened up here, for three entire days. After that, you can say what you want, but if you utter one word about your time here before the sun sets on the third day, you will die. She agreed, and Taquitz sent her home.

Everyone was amazed to see her. Where have you been? they asked, but instead of answering, she asked questions of her own. Father, why has your hair turned gray? Mother, where did those lines around your eyes come from? Brother, how have you grown so tall? Her family had no answers to her strange questions, and so three days passed in confusion. Then the sun set on the third day, and the girl told the people to build a large fire. Once everyone was gathered around the blaze, she stood before them and told everything she could remember and a few things she only thought she remembered: she spoke of Taquitz's lazy ways in bed, the rides across the night sky on his fiery back, the journey to the endless water into which the sun sizzled while boiled fish rose to the bubbling surface. She left nothing out, enjoying the telling and the rapt faces lit by firelight. That night, she slept well, but the next day a ray from the morning star turned hard as stone and pierced her like a spear. She dropped dead on the ground.

It wasn't anyone's fault, only a misunderstanding. How could anyone have known that a single day for Taquitz lasted an entire year for everyone else?

I left the library as night fell, bleary eyed and chuckling, happier than I'd been in months. I watched the city pass from the elevated train: old freight cars covered in fresh graffiti, a lonely monument to Dr. King, a defunct textile factory half transformed into yuppie lofts across the tracks from a tidy housing project. The sky was black with clouds about to break. I didn't know what to expect of winter in this part of the world. I got off at my station and climbed to a footbridge that crossed over the busy avenue. I stopped in the middle of the covered bridge, arrested by a sky like none I'd seen. The vivid orange light of sundown smoldered behind black clouds. The scene reminded me of a program I'd seen about volcanoes, how the lava's black crust cracked to show the molten gunk inside. I locked my fingers through the wires of the cage and settled in to watch. Skyscrapers rose to the north like glowing mountains. Cars came and went below, twin rivers, one white, the other red, flowing against each other. I stood there until the sky faded to the color of ash. Then I crossed to the other side of the street and walked back to my apartment.

Epilogue
Rock Island

Here I am, in a college classroom thirty years after Speech with Mr. Solter. I've come a long way, from the back of the class to the front, from middle school to college, from California to Illinois. As I type, the students of the term's last class scratch away at their final exam. The course, an introduction to contemporary literary fiction, fulfills a general education requirement. This time around, most of the students are pre-med, serious about earning their place in the world, anxious to get literature out of the way. I like them, the majority of them at least. It's hard not to, how earnestly they read the novels and stories I assigned them and which I love. They follow rules, try to be kind, to remind themselves to be grateful, and they expect to be rewarded for being good. I wonder what Solter would say to them.

Personally, I don't preach the gospel of no free lunches. I can certainly look back at my life and see instances of hard luck—usually stemming from bad decisions—but for every one of these cases, I can also find some gift, freely given. My grandparents taking me in when I was down and no good to anyone. The taxpayers of California offering me a second shot at higher education. All the lovers and friends who'd chosen to spend their time with me, and not someone else, time they will never get back. And then there are beaches, waves, mountains, defunct factories along the banks of the Mississippi, all free. Perhaps my students' expectations will be fulfilled, though probably not in the form they anticipate.

I hope it's not too much to ask that a handful of these students will actually turn to literature, to good stories, in their spare time as a result of this course and others like it, and that stories may make them better people in the long run, or help them through difficult times. This is to say that I like to believe that what I'm doing matters to someone other than myself. At the very least, all but the most forgetful of my students learn that periods and commas go inside, and not outside, quotation marks in written American English. A couple times a year, a student comes to me, struggling with some version of the question that had dogged me for so long: What to do?

I tend to suggest travel, and patience, anything but stagnation, anything but the path of least resistance. This is not much of a solution, I realize, but it's what I've got.

Looking out the window at the leafy, hilly campus, the grand old buildings, the meandering paths, I can hardly believe that I've landed here, of all places, on this campus in this post-industrial city on the Mississippi River, faded, rusting, and yet beautiful if you've got an eye for this sort of beauty. It took ten years, two degrees, and a place called Kalamazoo in between, to get from Atlanta to here. Perhaps there's a story in that decade, but I'm not so sure. It seems, looking back, that my course was set the moment I walked into Theories of Composition, and I followed it without many detours, as if I'd been wandering for years without a map, and then boarded a train; as long as I didn't get off along the way, I'd eventually arrive at the destination. And here I am.

Most everyone else is still in California. My mother is well, though poor. She finally had the operation, which helped, and she's still married to Ralph, though they currently live in separate residences—she in a trailer out in the desert, he in an apartment nearby. They've taught me that marriage comes in more forms than television and movies would lead us to believe. Mom is thinking about moving to San Diego to live with her sister, Annie. Jeremy's married with a son, making good money as a union carpenter. Ralph managed to retire from his latest job building and installing cabinets, and now he gets by playing bass in a rock band.

My father came upon an inheritance when Les died a few years back, and with the money he bought a new truck with a large camper on the bed. Frequently he sleeps in the parking lot of Crystal Cove, kept company by a shaggy little mutt he adopted, named Charlie. He still surfs. We talk on the phone once a year or so, and he helped me out with some money over the years, especially when I'd fallen into credit-card debt after school ended but before my job started. Later, on the occasion of my wedding—an intimate affair in one of the rocky coves of Laguna—he gifted me another stack of bills, money he certainly could have used for himself, and I'm grateful for that.

Ole's currently a free man, and what's more, he left California. I won't say where he's gone, because he split while still on probation—not that the authorities have the resources or desire to hunt down a run-of-the-mill probation violator. I understand he's trying to legally get out of the mess, so he can move to live near his son in another state. Over the years, he's become a skilled tattoo artist, and if he manages to stay off dope, he just might make it this time. I choose to believe he will.

Gil and Helen are alive and well. They sold Casa Three Arch and moved into a relatively modest home a couple miles inland in Laguna Niguel. Recent economic troubles and a medical situation have conspired to hurt them financially, and they've been forced to rent a spare room to a stranger. My mom, however, thinks they took in the boarder because it was the easiest way to keep my dad from moving back in whenever he got tired of sleeping in the camper. At any rate, I plan to visit one of these days, especially now that I have an infant son that everyone's anxious to meet. Time, as always, is short these days.

I'm impatient for the term to end, even more so than usual. It's spring, and the weather is fine. I'd always taken good weather for granted in California, but here such days are precious, and I've learned to appreciate them, to get outside no matter what else is going on. But the main reason I'm anxious to close the book on this term is that my wife and son are waiting for me in Italy. She's a citizen of that country and is currently introducing our boy to his Old-World relatives, and to the language, food, and culture there. Babies start eating pasta in Italy at four months. I guess some stereotypes hold true.

Someone who knows me well has recently suggested that I married a foreigner to reconcile two opposing desires. In this way I have managed to satisfy my wanderlust within the stabilizing confines of family. Perhaps this friend is right, though I'm not so sure. The truth is, I don't feel much like traveling these days. These days, I prefer to stay home.

ACKNOWLEDGMENTS

I would like to thank the MacDowell Colony for "the freedom to create" and Augustana College for the time.

I couldn't have written this book without the guidance of my teachers over the years, especially Richard Linder, Paul Bailiff, Pam Durban, John Holman, Jim Grimsley, Jaimy Gordon, Stuart Dybek, Naeem Murr, Richard Katrovas, and Robert Eversz.

Thanks to Gene Hayworth for plucking my manuscript from the slush pile.

I am grateful to Cody Todd and Rick Skwiot for reading a draft of the manuscript and offering invaluable advice.

Finally, I wish to thank my wife, Myriam Stangherlin, for everything.